Secret Coastline II

Secret Coastline II

MORE JOURNEYS AND DISCOVERIES ALONG BC'S SHORES

by Andrew Scott

whitecap

 For additional information, please contact Whitecap Books, 351 Lynn Avenue, North Vancouver, British Columbia, Canada V7J 2C4.

Edited by Elaine Jones
Proofread by Joan Tetrault
Interior page design by Marjolein Visser
Printed and bound in Canada by Friesens

Library and Archives Canada Cataloguing in Publication
Scott, Andrew, 1947–
Secret coastline 2 : more journeys and discoveries along B.C.'s shores / Andrew Scott.
ISBN 1-55285-662-3
1. Scott, Andrew, 1947– —Travel—British Columbia—Pacific Coast. 2. Pacific Coast (B.C.)—Description and travel. 3. Pacific Coast (B.C.)—Biography. I. Title. II. Title: Secret coastline two.
FC3845.P2S363 2005 971.1'05 C2004-907078-9

The publisher acknowledges the financial support of the Government of Canada through the Book Publishing Industry Development Program for our publishing activities.

Contents

Coastal Map of British Columbia
LAX KW'ALAAMS
PORT EDWARD
GRAHAM
ISLAND
QUEENS SOUND
NAMU
RIVERS INLET
KNIGHT INLET
GLENDALE COVE
JERVIS INLET
DESOLATION
SOUND
QUADRA & CORTES ISLANDS
SAVARY ISLAND
HOWE SOUND
TEXADA ISLAND
BALLENAS-WINCHELSEA
n
GULF
ISLANDS
SECHELT INLET
0KM
200KM

Acknowledgements

In the course of researching twenty-four stories, I met many amazing people—far more than I can easily mention here. For assistance received, however, I'd particularly (and alphabetically) like to thank Mike Allegretti, Tamsin Baker and her colleagues at The Land Conservancy of BC, Irvin Banman, Patricia Banning-Lover of the Wild Bird Trust of BC, Dianne Bersea, Jim and Mary Borrowman of Stubbs Island Whale Watching, Daniel Bouman, Ron Breadner, Delores Broten, Randy Burke of Bluewater Adventures, Wayne Campbell, Sophie Cormier of the North Pacific Cannery Village Museum, John Dafoe, Garry and Carol Ehman, Dr. John Field, Elaine Futterman, Tony Greenfield, Katrin Gross, Dr. Michael Jackson, Patricia Keays, Ralph and Lannie Keller of Discovery Islands Lodge, Lori Kemp, Eddie and Karen Knott, Bruce and Dulcie Macdonald, Mike Preston, Dr. Wilf Schofield of the University of British Columbia botany department and Dr. Roland Stull of UBC's earth and ocean sciences department.

For background material on coastal BC I am indebted to numerous local writers and editors, especially Bill Wolferstan for his *Cruising Guide to BC* series; Betty Keller and Rosella Leslie for *Bright Seas, Pioneer Spirits*; Kenneth Campbell for *North Coast Odyssey*; Peter McGee for *Kayak Routes of the Pacific Northwest Coast*; Ian Kennedy for *Sunny Sandy Savary*; Doreen Armitage for *Around the Sound*; and Daniel Francis for the *Encylopedia of British Columbia*.

Katherine Johnston was by my side (or slightly ahead of me) on most of these journeys. I thank her especially for her fine company, wise counsel and loving support.

Foreword

This collection of stories about the British Columbia coast got its start—as did *Secret Coastline,* its predecessor—mainly in the pages of the *Georgia Straight.* I've been writing, on and off, for Vancouver's near-immortal weekly newspaper for thirty-one years. I've had a monthly column there for the past eleven years. Since January 1998, this column has been called "Coastlines."

I thank the editors I've been fortunate to work with at the *Straight*—Beverley Sinclair (now at *Shared Vision*), Ian Hanington, John Burns, Martin Dunphy, Nick Rockel, John Masters—and I also thank Anne Rose, editor of *Westworld* magazine, where additional segments of this book first came into being. I hasten to add that all the pieces in *Secret Coastline II* are substantially different from anything you may have seen before. The stories are longer, to begin with. A newspaper column is perfect for a quick peek at a topic but rarely adequate for a deeper examination. Ideas that appeared first in periodical form are here fully developed, filled in and brought up to date.

Secret Coastline II explores BC's coastal culture: its geography and history, its wild and human communities. It's often, but not always, about travel—especially by kayak, my preferred mode of transportation. The first *Secret Coastline*, published in 2000, had a section of profiles, "Faces of the Coast," and one on boats, "By Way of Water." In this volume, the faces are everywhere; stories throughout the book have strong biographical elements. Boats are seen mainly from a paddler's perspective.

An underlying theme of the book is ecotourism, which was the title of my original *Georgia Straight* column. In the '90s, the more I wrote on the subject the more amorphous and hard-to-pin-down it became. Ecotourism meant too many things to too many people (jetboats? helicopters?), and I eventually abandoned the column in frustration. Tourism is two-faced: it can support an economy and provide jobs, but it can also disrupt communities and destroy the environment. Because it promises to winkle out every last beauty spot and send a human cargo there, the industry needs a degree of control.

Even low-impact ecotourism at its best—unmotorized, locally owned and staffed, with "green" operations and an educational component—can have negative effects, especially if it expands in a poorly planned and unregulated fashion. Still, I'm convinced that sustainable ecotourism can play a useful role in BC's coastal culture. The number of kayakers on the coast, for instance, has increased greatly over the past decade, and they are a tourist crowd worth attracting: responsible, aware and relatively affluent. They must have toilets, however, and they can easily overwhelm fragile habitats, such as small islands. Kayaking quotas will soon be required for certain parts of the coast, with online registration for users. In other areas, future carrying capacities for paddlers will have to be determined.

Tourism, though sometimes harmful, has one redeeming quality: it has the capability to protect. Tourism cannot succeed unless there's something worth touring; it brings with it one more reason to keep our coastal paradise as unspoiled as possible.

British Columbia is a fertile haunt if you have an interest in natural history. And it's a grand place to visit, for the same reason. In this section I touch on many aspects of the natural world: plants, birds, fish, and marine and land mammals. Sorry, but I couldn't squeeze in crustaceans or insects.

BC has its share of endangered creatures, and many of these stories focus on species in peril. But there are also tales of promise: the encouraging increase of interest in birdwatching, the reclaiming of ancient habitats by humpback whales. Even in the case of threatened animals and plants, I've emphasized what can be done—and what is being done—to protect and restore. Canada's new Species at Risk Act, and the recovery teams that the act is setting in motion, are bringing glimmers of light to the conservation horizon.

To choose just six nature stories is a travesty, I know. If it's any consolation, preserving wilderness is a theme that runs throughout this book. Other chapters—especially "Paddling with Wolves" and "Texada's Sticklebacks"—also delve into natural history topics.

Natural History

A SUNSHINE COAST MOSS GARDEN NEAR HALFMOON BAY

Mostly Mosses

Wilf Schofield gets our noses to the ground

We like our coastal wildlife symbols large in British Columbia: killer whales, spirit bears, old-growth giants of red cedar and Sitka spruce. But there are other classes of living creatures—tiny, wondrous beings varied and spectacular in shape and form—that are as representative of BC as any whale or bear. I'm thinking here, particularly, of the mosses that carpet our forest floors and eclipse the rocks and trees with their verdant textures.

The BC coast, in fact, is one huge moss garden. After walking in the woods, the images that linger in my mind include the great trees, to be sure, but also the feathery, virescent strands that hang from the branches of those trees, the woven mats of vegetation that seem to upholster all visible surfaces, and the miniature emerald jewels sprouting from every fallen log.

More than 75 percent of Canada's 965 species of moss are found in BC. One hundred and sixty BC mosses are not found elsewhere in Canada; a number of species, in fact, are endemic, meaning they are found nowhere else in the world. Mosses, along with their liverwort and hornwort cousins, are known as bryophytes. The few botanists who specialize in them are bryologists.

The dean of Canadian bryologists—and a treasure house on the subject of BC mosses—is retired University of British Columbia (UBC) professor Wilf Schofield. Dr. Schofield's Introduction to Bryology is the standard textbook on the subject, and his Some Common Mosses of British Columbia, republished in a new edition in 1992 by the Royal British Columbia Museum, is indispensable for learning more about local plants. He is also the co-author of several books on plant evolution and has a long list of periodical publishing credits.

A legendary collector, Schofield has discovered several new moss species, which now, of course, bear his name. Almost half the specimens in UBC's herbarium, which occupies the top floor of the biology building, are bryophytes, making the moss collection, neatly arrayed on metal shelves in thousands upon thousands of cardboard shoeboxes, one of the largest in North America. Of the 230,000 moss specimens, Schofield personally gathered 117,000. That averages out to eight per day, every day, over the course of a forty-year collecting career.

One bright spring morning I travel to UBC to meet the eminent scientist, visit the herbarium and sit in on a class and laboratory session at the botany department. I work my way deep into the maze of hallways and annexes at the heart of the biological sciences complex, past the "Caution! Fungal Pathogens" sign, and finally locate Schofield's office. Any trepidations I have about interviewing so distinguished a person are soon put to rest; the master of moss turns out to be a friendly, outgoing sort who quickly welcomes me to his computer-free lair. A presence on the Point Grey campus since 1960, he is lean and spry at seventy-six and still lectures on occasion, as he will do today.

The walls of his office are covered with books, some very old and beautiful. Schofield pulls out a rare volume of *Bryologia Europa*, a series published in Latin, French and German in Stuttgart in the 1850s, and shows me its fine illustrations of mosses. Several boxes are strewn around, labelled "Attu," fruit of a recent collecting foray to Alaska. Zeiss and Nikon microscopes await a series of bagged and labelled specimens. Many surfaces in the room are decorated with a healthy sprinkling of dust, soil and dried plant fibres. My host is nothing if not down to earth.

He is also extremely modest about his accomplishments. "I respond emotionally to bryophytes," he tells me, "thus I'm probably not really a scientist." In truth, he combines an unbounded curiosity about the natural world with a passionate commitment to teaching. "What I love most," he says, "is passing on knowledge." This he has done well; many of North America's leading bryologists are former students of Wilf Schofield.

After our interview, I accompany the professor to a nearby botany lab. There, under his tutelage and that of lecturer Shona Ellis, thirty students and I slip into an intriguing world of bizarre miniature lifeforms. Within our forests, I discover, are other, smaller forests, equally tangled and impenetrable: groves of *Polytrichum*, undulating plantations of *Neckera*, twisted thickets of *Heterocladium*.

Even with a modest hand lens we can easily examine the individual "trees" in these jungles. A powerful microscope, though, brings their fronds and tendrils and leafy starbursts to eye-boggling proximity. The moist green parts of moss plants are known as gametophytes; they grow the minute male or female sex organs. The male organs produce sperm cells that actually swim along the wet branches of moss to fertilize tiny female eggs. But then, explains Schofield, the moss life cycle takes an unexpected turn.

The fertilized egg, or zygote, puts out a long, thin stalk, the seta, with a swollen tip that develops into a storage container for spores. This entire body is called a sporophyte, and it is dependent on the gametophyte for water and nutrients. When the swollen tip, or sporangium, is mature, a tiny cap forms, then breaks off when the capsule dries out. Sporangia come in myriad unusual shapes. At extreme magnification one could imagine them as miniature alien space pods. When the cap falls away, a strange ring of moisture-responsive teeth becomes visible. The teeth pulsate in such a fashion that individual spores are transferred out of the sporangium and then carried off by air or water to start new colonies.

Our teachers point out that the gametophytes are equally varied in shape and style, with leaves that are ribbed or pleated, dull or shiny, sleek or wrinkled, smooth or serrated. They come in a range of colours: black, red, orange, purple and yellow, as well as green. Mosses not only reproduce sexually, they can also propagate from broken fragments and from specialized cell masses called gemmae, which grow at the leaf tips and then break off to form new plants. With all these reproductive means at their disposal, it's not hard to see how they manage to cover as much ground as they do.

The common names given to mosses, while they may not have much scientific acceptance, do help convey a sense of enormous diversity. We have hair, haircap, hairy lantern, crane's-bill, cord, cat-tail, thread, badge and fan mosses. There are plume, tangle, spear, cotton, bristle, bottle, pipecleaner, roof, stair step and screw mosses. Some species are named after their leaves: bent, coiled, beaked, blunt, goose-necked, lanky, thatched, hanging and rough. For romantics, there's lover's moss and goblin's gold. And who could forget any plant with the name of Menzies' red-mouthed mnium?

At the end of my UBC visit, Schofield kindly offers to take a trip in the near future to the Sunshine Coast, where I live, and lead a small group on a moss-hunting expedition. I jump at this chance, round up half a dozen eager, nature-loving friends and, a few weeks later, the generous professor makes a house call.

We set off by foot toward the surrounding forest but, before covering even twenty metres, stop several times beside the road and identify a dozen different species of moss. In the nearby woods we scramble around cliffs and into swamps and gullies, our noses rarely more than twenty centimetres from the ground. Dog-walking neighbours can only assume that we've lost something: our minds, perhaps. Every few steps, Schofield relates some details of bryological lore: how mosses lack complex vascular systems, for instance, and absorb water and nutrients directly through stems and leaves; how some species become dormant when rainfall is low, then resume activity after a good soaking.

After the tour, over a bag lunch back on my outdoor deck, our guide tells us about the history of moss research in BC, which started with Archibald Menzies aboard the fur-trading vessel *Prince of Wales* in 1787. Menzies, a surgeon, also collected mosses on Captain George Vancouver's voyages in the early 1790s. Dominion Botanist John Macoun made important early collections of BC mosses between 1872 and 1916.

Schofield tells us about his own gathering expeditions, which have focused in recent years on the Queen Charlottes and on some of the most difficult-to-reach islands in Alaska's Aleutian chain. He hasn't let retirement interfere with writing and publishing, either. His latest work, which appeared in 2002, is a *Field Guide to Liverwort Genera of Pacific North America*.

Many people see moss as a mere nuisance, something to be eradicated from driveway or roof with an expensive bottle of chemical plant killer. This viewpoint must change, according to Wilf Schofield, if the scarcer mosses are to survive. Over one hundred species are imperilled by logging, agriculture, urban development and climate change. Most bryophytes, for instance, are very sensitive to air pollution, and numerous Lower Mainland mosses are especially affected. Some species are only found in our rapidly declining old-growth forests. Several, such as *Bryhnia hultenii*, may already have been extirpated from BC by logging activity. Others, like the tiny *Fissidens pauperculus*, which Schofield has lovingly watched over for three decades in its Lynn Canyon home, are hanging on at only one known location in the province. "I'm always on the lookout," he says, "but I've never seen it elsewhere in British Columbia. If we lose this patch then that may be it for Canada."

Perhaps the biggest threat to bryophytes is human ignorance. Because they are small and subtle, unlike killer whales and spirit bears, they are easily overlooked. Many consider them insignificant and unimportant. But we need mosses. They break down rock surfaces to begin the all-important process of soil creation and make minerals available to plants as nutrients. Their sponge-like capacity to hold water helps slow runoff and prevent erosion.

The Pacific dogwood is BC's provincial flower; the Steller's jay is our provincial bird. We have an official tree (western red cedar) and an official mineral (jade). We even have a provincial tartan, for goodness' sake. Perhaps now is the time to think small and become the first Canadian province to adopt an official bryophyte. The call for nominations is open.

TWO HUMPBACK WHALES REST BETWEEN DIVES AT DRANEY NARROWS.

Return of the Humpbacks

Round Rivers Inlet on the Gikumi

Moses Inlet is a long, beckoning finger in the heart of the coastal rainforest. The landscape here is rugged: granite bluffs soar above black waters. On an afternoon in late October, the seventeen-metre *Gikumi* is cruising up the narrow fjord under a canopy of low cloud. There are four of us aboard: Jim and Mary Borrowman, who own the rebuilt, fifty-year-old tug, my partner, Katherine Johnston, and me. We're searching for humpback whales.

There have been recent reports of humpbacks in the area, especially where Moses joins Rivers Inlet about eighty kilometres south of Ocean Falls and four hundred kilometres northwest of Vancouver. We, however, have seen nothing—and no one. About halfway up Moses Inlet, near where it takes a jog to the east, we finally spy a small boat, its dark colours almost indistinguishable against the backdrop of forest and cliff. The vessel's operator appears to be sneaking a few illicit logs off a steep hillside. We stop to ask if he's seen any whales in the neighbourhood.

"You should have been here last week," the pirate logger cheerfully replies. "There were dozens of humpbacks in the inlet. They were splashing the surface with their tails and their fins, jumping out of the water everywhere. I wasted a whole day watching them."

We groan in dismay; we'd be thrilled to waste our time this way.

Almost forty years after a ban on hunting in the North Pacific, humpback sightings are on the increase off BC's shores. The gigantic mammals, once driven to near-extinction by relentless commercial whaling, are returning to their ancient haunts. Future ferry passengers may even see breaching whales in the Strait of Georgia and near BC's main urban centres. Scientists are trying to gather as much information as they can about the species in order to help in its recovery. And they've enlisted the aid of observers, such as the Borrowmans, up and down the coast.

Based at Telegraph Cove on Vancouver Island, Mary and Jim are whale-watching pioneers and enthusiasts. From May to September, their Stubbs Island tour company takes thousands of people into Johnstone and Queen Charlotte straits in order to see killer whales, dolphins, porpoises, sea lions and the occasional larger whale. They are mad about marine mammals, so much so that the genial, ginger-haired Jim even collects them, or what's left of them, after they've died and decayed.

He's a bone man. Above the entrance to his business is a killer whale skeleton with its jaws, full of wicked-looking pointy teeth, aimed at prospective customers. Strewn about the wharf are the remains of minke, sperm and gray whales. "Finny," the pride of the collection, was a wedding gift from Mary, who decided she would humour her husband-to-be's eccentricities. Finny is a rarity in BC waters, a seventeen-metre fin whale, which had the misfortune to be impaled on the bow of a cruiseship and carried to Vancouver. Now Finny's skull and vertebrae are on display. "The rest of him," Jim explains, when we stop by for a visit, "is in the freight shed," along with a dozen or more other creatures, from sea otters to dolphins. "The small bits are in buckets," Borrowman adds. His latest acquisition is an even rarer visitor to BC: a pygmy sperm whale. The goal of this singular hobby is to display the articulated skeletons at Telegraph Cove's expanding marine museum.

In the off-season, besides working to develop the centre, the Borrowmans cruise north with the *Gikumi*, which was once the workboat at Telegraph Cove's long-defunct lumber mill. They take identification photos of whales and do whatever else they can to contribute to marine mammal research. When they invite us to go along for a few days, we naturally jump at the chance. Now we're dodging winter's first storms on the central BC coast, binoculars pressed to our faces, waiting to spot the filmy spout of water vapour that announces the presence of *Megaptera novaeangliae*.

Humpbacks and grays are BC's predominant large whales. The grays, hunted in the North Pacific until 1936, seem to have regained their pre-whaling population of 20,000 to 25,000. Humpbacks have been slower to recover; whaling for this species was not banned until 1965, and an illegal Russian hunt continued until 1980.

Both species migrate stupendous distances to winter breeding grounds. The grays go to Baja. Most of BC's humpbacks head to Hawaii to mate and bear their young, while a few may trek south to Mexican and Costa Rican waters or even swim all the way to breeding areas off Japan. As with the grays, some North Pacific humpbacks don't migrate at all, preferring to spend the entire winter contentedly feeding in their traditional summer range, which stretches from California to Alaska and the Bering Sea.

Stocks of humpbacks are encountered in most of the world's oceans. In the North Atlantic, the whales feed off Nova Scotia, Greenland and Iceland, then migrate to Caribbean waters to breed and calve. A small group in the Arabian Sea appears to stay put in tropical waters all year-round. Migration patterns in the southern hemisphere are less well understood, but stretch between the frigid waters lapping Antarctica and the coasts of southern Africa, South America and Australia.

Unlike gray whales, BC's humpbacks regularly feed up the inlets, as well as off the coast. While travelling to Bella Coola on BC Ferries' *Queen of Chilliwack*, I've spotted individual animals in the distance in Fitz Hugh Sound and way up Dean Channel. The Strait of Georgia once supported a substantial population. "The *Douglas* reports the waters near Deep Bay at the entrance to Baynes Sound alive with humpbacks," announced Victoria's *British Colonist* in 1868, "hundreds being seen both going up and coming down."

Humpbacks trap food by filtering water through a thick fibrous substance called baleen that hangs from the roofs of their mouths. They seem fairly adaptable in terms of what they can eat, which may contribute to their wide-ranging explorations—and to their ongoing recovery. Off BC, they're known to feed on tiny shrimplike euphausiids, or krill, as well

A GRUMMAN GOOSE SEAPLANE DEPOSITS US
AT THE DAWSONS LANDING FLOAT IN RIVERS INLET.

as on herring, pilchard and sand lance. Not surprisingly, any changes to the populations of these small schooling fish could have grave consequences for the whales.

"What the humpbacks do have going for them," says Jim Darling, one of BC's leading whale researchers, "is that if it's a poor year for, say, pilchard, they can potentially shift to another food item. That's the theory, anyway." Darling, a gray-whale specialist, who also spends half the year in Hawaii studying the role that "singing" plays in humpback behaviour, emphasizes that no specific studies have yet been done on humpback prey in BC. "Shifts in prey," he suggests, "could well be responsible for humpbacks moving inshore."

Like killer whales, individual humpbacks can be distinguished by their markings. Darling participates in a photo-recognition project coordinated by the National Marine

Mammal Laboratory in Seattle. Killer whales are identified by their dorsal fins and the grey "saddle patch" on their backs. For humpbacks, it's the undersides of the flukes that are characteristic: the mottled blacks and whites, plus any nicks and scrapes, tell the tail.

The Seattle lab uses image-processing software to compare new tail photos against the more than 25,000 already on file, thus keeping track of known whales while adding new IDs to its database. By 1999, researchers had identified over 3,100 individual humpbacks in the North Pacific. Current North Pacific population estimates vary wildly, from 6,000 to 15,000 animals, up dramatically from 1,000 in 1966. Trying to arrive at a global figure for the species is difficult; there may be as many as 20,000 to 40,000 whales in total, about 10 to 20 percent of their original numbers before commercial exploitation.

Killer-whale expert John Ford, who left the Vancouver Aquarium in 2001 to direct marine mammal research at Nanaimo's Pacific Biological Station, points out that 60 percent of BC humpbacks have all-black tails and can only be distinguished by indentations along the edge of the fluke. The Nanaimo station, operated by Fisheries and Oceans Canada, also has thousands of humpback tail photos, many taken off the north coast of Haida Gwaii by biologist Graeme Ellis. Station staff are analyzing the images and plan to produce a humpback catalogue. "We're still in the early stages," Ford cautions. "It's quite time-consuming going through all these photos, picking the best flukes, scanning, printing and matching them. We don't really know yet how many humpbacks we have in BC waters, but I would say at least 500 individuals."

We fly into Rivers Inlet by float plane to join the Borrowmans at Dawsons Landing. The flight north from Port Hardy, on a rare clear day, is a dazzling experience. Several hundred Pacific white-sided dolphins skip across the waves below us as we swoop over Queen Charlotte Strait. A pair of humpback whales—a harbinger of future sightings?—is clearly visible swimming just beneath the surface.

At first glance, Dawsons seems a strange place to establish a community, however small. There are few building sites in the dark, protected canyon of Darby Channel. But this is a floating village; all it needs is good moorage and shelter from the weather. We make an obligatory tour of Rob and Nola Bachen's rambling, green-and-white general store and post office, with its clothing section, tools, used books, souvenirs and vast marine supply, fishing gear and liquor departments. "Sometimes people find things here they've been looking for for years," Jim says. A fuel station and a handful of homes and sheds comprise the rest of Dawsons, which is surrounded by dripping docks where several floating fish lodges are tied up, safe from the notorious pounding the region receives in winter.

A day later, after exploring Moses Inlet, we're concentrating our search on the east side of Rivers Inlet. Ensconced in the *Gikumi's* cozy wheelhouse and fortified by another of Mary's fine seafood lunches, we come level with the old Good Hope cannery, now reincarnated as luxurious King Salmon fishing lodge. I notice something unusual—a momentary plume of whitish vapour—in the distance, off Florence Island. It could be the spouting of a whale. Our adrenalin kicks in. Then we spot two more blows near Wadhams, another old cannery site. Things are happening at last.

Humpbacks for sure, says Jim—at least three, perhaps more. We get a quick peek at a broad black back and small dorsal fin before the first whale submerges. The others are quite far away, moving west across the mouth of Johnston Bay. Suddenly, one whale breaches, staggering us as it leaps almost completely out of the water. I watch through binoculars as its huge body floats for a second, suspended in air, then falls back with an enormous explosion of spray. I can make out the whale's long dangling pectoral fins (*megaptera* means "big wing") and its greyish belly. There's another breach, then another, half a dozen in all.

We catch up with the jumpers—two adults and a large calf—and follow them along the shoreline at a respectful distance. It's good watching weather: dry, cloudy, calm. At the entrance to Draney Inlet the whales pause. Will they go in? The tide is flooding; Draney Narrows is alive with eddies and small standing waves. The whales head toward the inlet and we follow.

Just inside the narrows, where the restless waters are churning, the whales appear to feed. We drift, engine off, and see that there are five animals in total. Many birds are gathered, too: glaucous-winged gulls, common murres, western grebes. Tiny fish are jumping, but we can't tell what kind. Jim throws a hydrophone over the side and we listen as one whale makes a low roar, a sound Borrowman says he's never heard before.

As we watch the humpbacks, our hosts mark up a logbook provided by the BC Cetacean Sightings Network, a collaborative project of the Pacific Biological Station and the Vancouver Aquarium. The network enables boaters—professional mariners, especially—to contribute sightings to a growing database, which scientists are using to study distribution, migration and feeding patterns, and to estimate populations.

THE *GIKUMI* AT REST AT THE HEAD OF MOSES INLET

The whales come close. We can see their eyes and the knobs, or tubercles, on their heads that may reduce drag and make them more manoeuvrable as they swim. We can see their twin blowholes, almost like human nostrils, and the pleated throats that expand to hold vast volumes of water. The whales expel it through the baleen with their tongues, leaving behind some of the tonne or more of prey that each animal must consume daily. Humpbacks are often infested with prodigious quantities of barnacles, whale lice and worms, but we notice few of these external parasites.

Jim and I venture off in the *Gikumi's* skiff, hoping to position ourselves for good fluke shots. Borrowman—an experienced professional photographer whose stunning orca images, often taken while he's actually in the ocean with the whales, have enlivened many a magazine cover—uses a 300-millimetre lens and superfast black-and-white film in the fading light. Viewed from behind, the bulk and girth of the humpbacks are awesome. They are like swimming school buses: fourteen metres long, thirty-five tonnes in weight. In our open craft I feel as fragile as a porcelain doll.

Moist, fishy whale breath drifts over us. It's not nearly as foul as my reading ("a most detestable rank and poisonous stench," according to naturalist Johann Forster, who travelled with Captain James Cook) has led me to expect. The odour must depend on what the whales are eating. They surface beside us and spout three times before disappearing. Because they are buoyant with body fat, they must dive steeply to gain depth, which is why their flukes usually emerge from the water as they descend. One breath, two, three—here comes the colossal tail, wide as a double garage. I gape in nervous astonishment. Borrowman clicks away.

The whales we see are likely lunge feeding: charging through congregations of prey with open mouths. Their white pectoral fins could aid them in this; small fish may see a dark space between approaching white bars and head toward it to escape, only to be devoured. But humpbacks gather food in more complex ways, too. They "flick" feed, for instance, moving their tails back and forth at the surface to send a plume of spray forward that concentrates krill along its edge. The whale then gulps its meal from beneath.

The most impressive technique, a specialty of the humpbacks of northern BC and Alaska, is called "bubblenet" feeding. One whale swims beneath a school of prey fish, usually herring, and produces a large ring, or net, of bubbles that the fish try to avoid. Another whale makes loud "trumpet" calls to help herd the prey. As the fish bunch together, the whales rocket up, one by one (always in the same order), through the centre of the bubble cylinder, turning the surface of the sea into a cauldron of frenzied activity.

A bubblenet session can employ from three to twenty-four individuals. The procedure requires an unusual degree of co-operation, notes Fred Sharpe, a researcher with Simon Fraser University and the Alaska–BC Whale Foundation. Whales that feed this way, though not necessarily related, often develop long-term associations. Certain animals seem to lead, setting the nets, making the calls.

"We have a unique population of whales off this coast," Sharpe says. "They've broken out of their normal behavioural mode. They demonstrate communal tool use, acoustic manipulation of their prey and task specialization. They operate in large stable groups and form enduring bonds that can last for decades. The only other mammal with a similar social structure is the human being. These are probably the most unusual humpbacks in the world."

Place names along the BC shoreline, and especially in the Strait of Georgia, testify to the province's long association with whales. Within just a few leagues of Vancouver, we find Whale Passage, Whaling Station Bay (on Hornby Island), Whaletown (on Cortes Island), Blubber Bay (on Texada Island), two Whalebone points, the Ballenas Islands and Channel, and Whaler Bay (on Galiano Island). Most of these names refer specifically to humpback whales.

The formerly abundant humpbacks prompted a strange mixture of attraction and fear on the part of local residents. They were always "disporting themselves" and "saucily spouting," according to reports in the *British Colonist* in the 1860s. But this captivation with whales and enjoyment of their antics was usually offset by a darker perspective: often "they were rather more playful than was agreeable or safe," and sometimes the whales were "monsters" who "spouted their defiance" at puny human observers.

On the west coast of Vancouver Island, the hunting of baleen whales was once a vital part of Nuu-chah-nulth First Nation culture. Commercial whaling by European and US ships commenced in the Pacific Northwest in the 1830s, but it wasn't until 1866, when James Dawson harpooned (but could not land) three humpbacks in Saanich Inlet, that a shore-based industry was ventured.

Between 1866 and 1873, at least eighty-one humpbacks were killed in the Strait of Georgia and Howe Sound. They were butchered for their oil, which was in demand for lamps and lubrication. Some baleen, used mainly in corset-making, was also harvested. Then the local industry collapsed.

By the early 1900s the whales had recovered, and the whalers, armed with faster ships and powerful harpoon guns, were back. Victoria's Pacific Whaling Company built a station at Page's Lagoon, just north of Nanaimo, in 1907. That winter, in just three months, ninety-seven humpbacks were killed from two steam vessels, the *Orion* and the *St. Lawrence*. The carcasses were converted to oil, leather, fertilizer and "whale-bone" (baleen). By the spring of 1908, the great inshore humpback hunt was over. The whales were finished. Humpbacks were not spotted again in the Strait of Georgia until 1976. Since then sightings have been rare. The pursuit continued elsewhere off the coast, however, for almost sixty years; between 1905 and 1965 more than 28,000 humpbacks were slaughtered in the North Pacific.

Perhaps today we can console ourselves with our new-found attitudes toward whales. Now, instead of threatening or frightening those who view them, humpbacks enthrall us with their grace, intelligence and playfulness. We may merely be projecting human characteristics onto the animals, but consider the experience of BC artist Stewart Marshall, who makes long journeys in a hand-built kayak to search out remote painting sites.

Marshall encountered a humpback calf and its mother several kilometres offshore in Queen Charlotte Sound. At first, from a distance, he thought they were in trouble, perhaps entangled in a fishing net. But when he got closer, he found a more reassuring scene. "They were playing in a gigantic floating kelp bed, lollygagging around, lying on their backs and running long kelp strands along their fins, scratching or tickling themselves. They knew I was there, but they carried on anyway for half an hour while I watched them." Other observers have seen individuals pushing logs back and forth with their heads. Whale polo, anyone?

Much of the current human love affair with humpbacks is associated with the sounds they make. This species has an amazing vocal range: low-frequency moans and snores, high-frequency chirps and cries, plus all kinds of utterances—"ees" and "woos" and "yups"—that change frequency. Recent research has focused on the long, rhythmic songs performed by males during breeding season— supposedly the most complex vocalizations in the animal kingdom after those of our own species.

All the adult males in one region sing the same song. In another ocean, the males will sing something quite different. A typical song lasts for ten to thirty minutes and is then repeated, often for hours at a time. Scientists are fascinated by

GOOSE BAY CANNERY, RIVERS INLET

the fact that the songs gradually change from year to year. The whales are "inveterate composers," according to US biologist Roger Payne. Payne has compared the patterns in humpback songs to human musical traditions and found the regular repetition of phrases and rhythms "strikingly similar."

Nobody knows the exact purpose of humpback song, though it's thought to be a form of sexual display. Female humpbacks may be attracted to the best singers, and the best singers may be males with novel songs or those capable of improvising on a basic melody.

Australian scientists recently set the marine-mammal community on its ear by demonstrating that two lost or visiting humpbacks from the Indian Ocean had, in less than two years, prompted all the male whales in the western Pacific to completely change their song, a process that would otherwise only have occurred in slow, cautious stages over decades. Could the whales be influenced by novelty, the scientists asked, in the same way that a catchy foreign tune might suddenly become the rage? Or perhaps they had to win the females' attention away from the fascinating newcomers.

This song-changing episode and the humpback's co-operative bubble-feeding behaviour suggest that the whales may learn from one another. Social learning is certainly easier if you live for a long time (fifty to eighty years) and remain in a stable group, as many whales do. Can older whales teach survival tips to student whales? Animals that pass on knowledge to each other would seem to possess the fundamentals of culture.

After our close encounter with the five humpbacks in Draney Inlet the weather turns nasty. We're forced to pass many hours snugged to a rain-slick dock in Goose Bay, reading and playing cribbage in the *Gikumi's* shipshape cabin. Such is the nature of cetacean research.

This is no hardship for me, as it's a chance to absorb some of the heritage of Rivers Inlet, once synonymous with big spring salmon and millions of sockeye. Eighteen canneries operated here between 1882 and the mid-1950s, when the last one shut down. In 1996, after an alarming decline in sockeye stocks, the inlet was closed to commercial fishing. Sport fishing continues unabated, however, and a dozen or so lodges cater to wealthy tourists, mostly from Europe or the US, in search of giant chinook.

It's hard to imagine 10,000 people living and working at Rivers, as once was the case. Today several hundred individuals tend to the sport fishers' needs in summer. About sixty residents occupy the First Nation hamlet of Oweekeno, or Katit, on the Wannock River at the head of the inlet. A few locals, such as the occupant of a Draney Inlet floathome we pass, are itinerant. The movable building, with "PRIVATE" painted across it in giant letters, is attached to a primitive A-frame for yarding logs off the steep slopes all around.

We learn more about the area from Ken Gillis, the dean of Duncanby Landing, where we're tied up. He's stuck also. A former Kamloops lawyer, Gillis bought Duncanby in the early 1990s, when a steady parade of gillnetters dropped by for fuel and food and booze. Then came the commercial shutdown. Now he has to rely on summer tourists renting his cabins and patronizing his store and a small restaurant, named Jessie's Place after his black Labrador.

"I'm just hanging on here," Gillis laments, over a steak-and-prawn dinner aboard the *Gikumi*. "My wife couldn't stand the rain and the isolation. Now it's just me and Jessie." After a glass or two of red wine, Gillis, a self-proclaimed redneck, waxes eloquent about politics, business, his neighbours and the history of the inlet.

The fifteen-bed hospital at Brunswick Bay, founded by famed missionary doctor George Darby, is long gone, he explains. At Wadhams, once the inlet's focal point, only the pier is left. But the Goose Bay cannery, just south of Duncanby, is somewhat intact. Next day, with the caretaker's permission, we gingerly explore the cannery's collapsing pier and cavernous main building, constructed with massive old-growth posts, beams and planks.

Slippery, decaying boardwalks lead to bunkhouses, a mess hall and office, and the manager's former home. The office is like a small museum, full of manuals and catalogues, with records dating back to the 1930s. I flick through an old file cabinet; there are official notices from World War II, and Union Steamship invoices that list white passengers by name but note others as "Indian woman" or "Chinese man." A barely legible letter stamped "Oakalla Prison Farm" regrets that the writer wouldn't be working at the cannery that summer as he'd been "pinched" for selling liquor to juveniles.

Over my shoulder I think I hear for a moment the bustle of another age.

We get a break in the weather, and Jim decides it would be prudent for us to dash south to Port Hardy before the *Gikumi* and her crew are locked any longer into Rivers Inlet by another extended session of wind and rain. While we travel we scan the horizon with our binoculars, searching anxiously for one last look at whales and wondering what the future holds for these marvellous, complex creatures.

Humpbacks, we realize, face many threats on their road to recovery. Hundreds have become trapped in fishing gear in the past twenty-five years, especially in the North Atlantic. Dozens have died as a result. (A federal disentanglement team is planned for the Pacific coast.) Fatal collisions with vessels are becoming more common; one occurred recently in Alaska's Glacier Bay, as did a near miss with a float plane. Humpbacks are at risk from pollutants and underwater noise disturbance: drilling, blasting, ship traffic and the US navy's low-frequency sonar (which could devastate many forms of marine life). And if the whales do recover, the Nuu-chah-nulth people have asserted their right to resume hunting them.

Will large baleen whales such as humpbacks ever again frequent heavily populated regions like the Strait of Georgia? "That would be wonderful," Jim Darling says, "but it depends entirely on the food situation." Scientists such as Darling and John Ford are encouraged by the humpbacks' increasing numbers, and Ford, in particular, will be developing publicly funded programs designed to continue the remarkable comeback.

Under the federal Species at Risk Act—inadequate though many conservationists and scientists believe it to be—Fisheries and Oceans Canada must devise recovery plans for endangered and threatened marine species. Government resources will be allocated according to need, meaning that northern right whales and southern resident orcas, which are in far the worst shape, will get priority. Humpbacks will be next in line, along with transient and northern resident orcas, all listed as threatened.

Preliminary research is already underway. There's the humpback catalogue, for instance. "We'll look at the timing of humpback movements to various parts of the coast," Ford says, "and at site fidelity, or how certain individuals come back to certain locations." Areas important for humpback feeding will be identified and prey stocks managed in a way that incorporates the whales' needs. The goal, Ford says, is nothing less than "getting humpback numbers back to their pre-whaling levels."

Clearly, the sight of humpbacks returning to BC waters fills most observers with hope and inspiration. Even though we see no more saucy spoutings as we slop our way across the exposed waters of Queen Charlotte Sound in the *Gikumi*, heading for the relative safety of Gordon and Goletas channels, there will, with luck, be whales to watch for on future journeys along the BC coast.

A CAUTIOUS GRIZZLY MAKES ITS WAY DOWN TO THE ARTIFICIAL SPAWNING CHANNELS ON THE GLENDALE RIVER.

Watching Grizzlies

With Barrie Gilbert at Glendale River

Two-year-old Panda and his 160-kilogram mother emerge from the bushes and walk directly beneath us on their way to the weir. For the next fifteen minutes they splash about in the water and catch half a dozen pink salmon, tearing out and eating the oil-rich eggs and brains before letting the carcasses float downstream, where they most assuredly will not go to waste.

At about seventy kilos, Panda is getting pretty big himself. With his large head, rounded ears and shaggy coat, he's fast becoming the very model of a handsome young grizzly bear. Next year he'll be on his own and may explore farther afield. But for now, these artificial spawning channels, built four kilometres up the Glendale River in 1989 by Fisheries and Oceans Canada, are a godsend for all grizzly cubs and their mothers—and there are still plenty of both—in this area of Knight Inlet, 250 kilometres northwest of Vancouver.

Breathless with excitement, we're watching the bears from an elevated viewing stand, with only a trapdoor between our tender flesh and all this ursine energy. The animals ignore our presence but treat the spawning channels with caution, their sensitive snouts held to the breeze to detect the presence of adult males, which sometimes eliminate future rivals by killing juveniles. There are eight of us in this stand, binoculars and cameras at the ready, including Ronna, a guide from nearby Knight Inlet Lodge, grizzly expert Dr. Barrie Gilbert, who teaches at Utah State University, and Owen Nevin from Northern Ireland, one of Gilbert's graduate students. The rest of our group is a short distance away in a second stand.

Over the course of two hours we see eight grizzlies at very close range. After Panda and his mom leave the site, a trio arrive: a pair of cute yearling cubs and their mother, nicknamed CJ by the local guides. They lumber over to a grassy patch right below the stand, where CJ tears up the ground with her gigantic paws and eats roots and leaves. The cubs climb into holes dug by other bears. Then they move to the river and leisurely devour spawning salmon for half an hour. CJ does all the work, while the cubs, whose fishing skills are still at the rudimentary stage, fight and play. After they wander farther downstream, a sub-adult bear shows up by itself. Later, two more three-year-old sub-adults pass through.

For us, this entire natural history lesson is but one stop on an amazing seven-day cruise of Knight Inlet, Johnstone and Queen Charlotte straits and the waters in between. Our home—or floating palace, I should say—is a twenty-one-metre ketch named *Island Roamer,* operated by Bluewater Adventures of North Vancouver. Skipper Ian Giles leads us safely through the waters, assisted by mate Neil Shearer.

TWO-YEAR-OLD PANDA AMUSES HIMSELF WHILE HIS MOTHER ENGAGES IN THE SERIOUS BUSINESS OF DEVOURING PINK SALMON.

We will see porpoises, sea lions and at least sixty killer whales on this voyage, including one massive male orca that swims right beneath the boat, clearly outlined in the translucent green water. A nine-metre-long minke whale surfaces beside us, while a group of fifteen Pacific white-sided dolphins join the *Roamer* for twenty minutes of bow-riding and acrobatic leaping. We pause at the derelict Kwakwaka'wakw village of Karlukwees. At abandoned Mamalilaculla on Village Island, Chief Tom Sewid gives us an animated tour; at the very live community of Alert Bay a visit to the astonishing masks of U'Mista Museum is in order.

Tonight the *Roamer* is tied up to Knight Inlet Lodge, a floating resort for sport fishers and wildlife watchers in Glendale Cove. We spend a relaxed evening aboard our vessel and enjoy paella, spinach and purple onion salad and corn on the cob. Pat Murray, the ship's superb cook, even finds time and space in her tiny galley to whip up a fancy cake to celebrate a fellow traveller's birthday. Next morning we'll be back at the lodge's viewing stands. Observing grizzlies is part of the package.

Dr. Gilbert is along, with his wife, Kathy, as an expert crew member to explain bear behaviour to us. He has come by his knowledge the hard way, losing an eye and suffering major facial damage during a grizzly bear attack at Yellowstone National Park in 1977. Considering the traumatic nature of this incident, it's surprising, perhaps, that Gilbert returned to studying bears after recovering from his injuries. But in fact, over the years, he has become a leading spokesman for their protection. Two of his graduate students are working at Glendale Cove this summer pursuing bear-oriented research.

Many wildlife scientists, including Barrie Gilbert, are completely opposed to the grizzly conservation approach of the current BC government, which overturned a moratorium on

CRUISING KNIGHT INLET ABOARD *THE ISLAND ROAMER*

grizzly hunting in 2001 and has done everything it can to prevent hunting data being made available to environmental organizations. He and his cohorts consider that the government's population estimates for BC of 10,000 to 13,000 grizzlies are vastly overstated. They believe that sport hunting and the continued erosion of forest habitat through clear-cutting and road-building is, in fact, having a serious negative effect on BC's grizzly bears.

Knight Inlet Lodge is pretty well the best place on the BC coast to safely watch and study grizzlies without disturbing

SKIPPER IAN GILES GIVES PASSENGERS A LESSON IN RAISING SAIL.

them. Moored at the site of a former fish cannery, the resort has been popular with sport fishers for several decades, though it's only since 1995, when Dean Wyatt purchased the place, that the focus has begun to shift toward wildlife viewing and ecotourism. The lodge is a jumble of floathouses, some modern and comfortable, others dating back to the 1940s. On the west side of the cove stand the ruins of a substantial logging camp.

Wyatt didn't know when he started out that bears would be a big part of his future. Because logging had silted up the Glendale's spawning beds and destroyed the salmon runs, grizzly populations had declined. The department of fisheries' channels did wonders for the salmon, though; now nearly half a million fish make their way upriver to spawn, fertilizing the forest and providing food for just about every creature in the neighbourhood. What's left over washes down into the estuary of the river to encourage a thick green growth of sedge, a protein-rich plant that grizzlies love to graze on when they emerge from their dens in the spring.

An environmental conference held at his lodge in 1996 convinced Wyatt to get involved in grizzly conservation. He established the Glendale Grizzly Trust Fund in order to allow scientists such as Barrie Gilbert to assess, from the very beginning, the effect of the wildlife viewing program on the bears and, if possible, help minimize its impact. Today, nearly all the 1,500 visitors a year who come to stay at the lodge do so for the unparalleled grizzly viewing.

For our second session, we're in the stands by eight a.m. Gulls, bald eagles, belted kingfishers and ravens are feasting on dead fish, as is a great blue heron, which chokes down, python-style, half a pink salmon. This effort takes several attempts; the tail-first approach is not the way to go, apparently. As we wait for bears, Nevin explains that his work is intended to help identify when and where the animals need to feed free of human disturbance. He and Gilbert hope to determine viewer limits for the site and how best to "time-share" the area between bears and people. They plan to map out river refuges where visitors may not go, as some bears are less tolerant of human presence than others. Ultimately, they want to develop a model for successful salmon-bear-tourist management that could be applied to other North American grizzly habitats.

The huge adult male bears, which can grow to 500 kilograms or more on the nutrient-rich BC coast, are very wary of humans, says Gilbert. He suspects that the females don't care much for us, either, but prefer our presence to that of the males. In effect, they use the tourists, who drive away the males, as a shield and a way to access the plentiful food supply in the spawning channels.

This morning we see fewer bears. Instead, we get to observe Panda and his mom for a long, uninterrupted period. After eating their fill of salmon they tussle together in the water for at least thirty minutes. It's wonderful to watch how patient the mother bear is with her toothy, somewhat rough offspring. Gilbert suggests that, as Panda has no siblings to play with, the mother may devote extra attention to him in this manner, helping him develop the coordination and confidence he'll need as an adult.

Next day we'll be heading home, so later that afternoon we leave Glendale Cove and cruise farther up Knight Inlet to Kwalate Creek for a last foray into the wild BC rainforest. Lodge employees (who usually carry pepper spray as a bear repellent, just in case) have built a fine trail here through thick undergrowth to a waterfall. We follow a tumbling stream filled with pink salmon, stopping often as we hike to examine the startling profusion of mosses and fungi. Our final wildlife sighting is a large black bear with lovely, light-coloured undermarkings, which retreats a safe distance into the woods, stands on a log, then regards us with baleful curiosity for a long, quiet, perfect moment.

RAINY DAY BIRDWATCHING AT THE SECHELT CHRISTMAS BIRD COUNT

The Age of Birding

Wayne Campbell, BC's leading ornithologist

At the front of the meeting hall sat a mysterious cage covered with heavy black cloth. Members of the Sunshine Coast Natural History Society milled around it, abuzz with what Wayne Campbell, BC's leading bird expert and the evening's scheduled speaker, appeared to have brought with him. Finally, after society president Tony Greenfield had brought the meeting to order, local naturalists Clint and Irene Davy took the podium. The cage, they announced, held a bird that Campbell had brought to their Gibsons Wildlife Rehabilitation Centre six months earlier and identified as a juvenile blue grouse. Tonight, they would unveil how his grouse had grown. Cliff then stepped back, flicked the cloth aside and revealed a very large, very tame barnyard turkey.

"That bird grew to forty pounds," adds Irene, today. "We called him Ricky, and he became a kind of ambassador for vegetarianism."

Months after the Sechelt meeting, I have a chance to visit Campbell and tour the Wild Bird Trust Wildlife Data Centre north of Victoria, an ambitious but short-lived project. Campbell chuckles when I remind him of the turkey story. Grouse and related species are difficult to tell apart when young, and he doesn't mind being proven wrong. A powerfully built figure with curly, graying hair and a mischievous grin, the sixty-two-year-old knows there are more important goals for a conservationist than mere identification.

Besides, when it comes to BC's birds, Campbell's contributions are unsurpassed. BC, a vital migration corridor, is home to 70 percent of Canada's 425 breeding bird species. The biologist is author or co-author of more than fifty books (including the encyclopedic, four-volume *Birds of British Columbia*); a long-time curator of ornithology at the Royal British Columbia Museum; recipient of the Order of BC and dozens of conservation awards; and a tireless advocate for wildlife.

Our airborne brethren need help, that's for sure; their habitat is decreasing as our population increases. A 2002 Audubon Society report estimates that one in four bird species in North America is in decline or at risk of disappearing altogether. Audubon officials continue to urge us to reduce pesticide use, grow more native plants in our yards and provide additional shelter and food for birds.

British Columbians, in particular, are responding. Since Campbell began his career, thousands of nature-oriented organizations have been formed in the province to revive wetlands, record data and pressure government and industry to improve conservation practices. Watching birds has never been more popular in BC than it is today. A recent survey concluded that nearly a third of North American adults—some 78 million enthusiasts throughout Canada and the US—are casual birdwatchers, and that they're spending $6.7 billion a year on bird-related goods and services. Of these, 26 million—up 265 percent since 1983—are serious birders. In fact, birding is North America's fastest-growing outdoor pursuit; bird festivals alone have soared from a dozen in the early 1990s to more than 200 continent-wide in 2005. It's that kind of energy and enthusiasm that Wayne Campbell and his fellow biologists are relying on as they ponder how this fascination might be harnessed for the benefit of the birds.

Katherine and I have become enthusiasts ourselves. How else to account for our regular presence at the Sunshine Coast's Christmas bird counts? Only a true enthusiast would continue to endure the varieties of winter weather that get thrown our way at these festive events.

The Sunshine Coast's "count circles," one in Sechelt and one in Pender Harbour, are two of about 2,000 in North America organized in late December by the National Audubon Society and Bird Studies Canada. The count got its start in 1900, when ornithologist Frank Chapman persuaded Audubon members to forgo a traditional US Christmas hunt and watch birds instead of shooting them. The idea caught on, to say the least. Last year, more than 50,000 birders enumerated almost 60 million birds, providing valuable baseline data for population and distribution studies. In BC, about seventy circles reported, with Delta bagging the highest number of species, at 140.

For a recent count we convene at eight a.m. in pelting rain at the Sechelt marsh, to be met by 75 mallards and 140 rock pigeons, all looking for handouts. The Sunshine Coast Natural History Society is sponsoring the day's activities, and our group of four is led by Tony Greenfield. Elsewhere in the district six other groups are spreading out to cover our twenty-four-kilometre-wide circle. At the end of the day everyone will meet for dinner to tabulate their results.

Greenfield is an ideal person to go birding with. Keen, but not fanatical, he has contributed for years to public education and conservation efforts on the Sunshine Coast. "Good spotting," he calls out cheerily whenever anyone sees an interesting bird—such as the great blue heron Katherine finds roosting in a Sitka spruce, or the belted kingfisher I catch a flash of at a neighbourhood pond.

Like many skilled birders, Greenfield can identify most species by song as well as by sight. "Listen," he prompts every few minutes. "Hear that?" First we focus on a tinny, nasal *anck, anck, anck* sound, one I detect all the time around my house. Now I know whose call it is: the red-breasted nuthatch. Then we catch the staccato *jip jip* of the winter wren and the high *see see see see* of golden-crowned kinglets. Large congregations of pine siskins swoop overhead, uttering soft, slurred buzzing calls.

By coffee time, we have a long list of the more common birds and are concentrating on some "good," or less obvious, species. At the golf course, where man-made, reed-fringed ponds bedevil local hackers but provide excellent bird habitat, we get an American coot. From a huge mixed flock of grazing Canada geese and American wigeons, Greenfield manages to pick out the brown head of a lone Eurasian wigeon—a good bird, for sure.

After stops at the dump (2,000 glaucous-winged gulls and a bald eagle) and Sechelt Inlet (a dozen species of waterfowl, including a lesser scaup and a pied-billed grebe), we head to a rural area where someone has noted owl activity. As we approach the treed site on foot, an orange and white barn owl bursts into the air and flaps silently away. This bird is better than good. New to the Christmas list, and only seen once before on the Sunshine Coast, it is a spectacular find, and more than makes up for the fact that Greenfield cannot coax a Virginia rail to return his excellent rail calls from a local cattail swamp. All in all, we see forty-seven species.

That evening, after a fine meal (turkey, not countable) and a few bottles of wine, a soggy but enthusiastic crew compare notes. The other groups have good birds, too: a saw-whet owl, a pileated woodpecker, six marbled murrelets, ten hermit thrushes, a sharp-shinned hawk. We end up with eighty-two species, way down from 1997's record of 102, but not bad considering the weather. We've had a grand time. And next week, at the Pender Harbour count, the truly dedicated will do it all over again.

In comparison to my recent conversion, Wayne Campbell came by his love of the natural world at a very early age. As a young child, he went on patrols with his grandfather, the first game warden at Alberta's Jasper National Park. "He taught me to look and to see," Campbell says. "That was the critical thing." The budding ornithologist also went hunting and fishing with his father. Later, after the family moved from Alberta to Burnaby, he found that his growing interest in conservation was dampening his willingness to kill. One day, out with his father on the Delta foreshore, he couldn't bring himself to fire at a duck flying overhead; he pretended that he hadn't seen the bird. His hunting days were over.

His birding days, however, were just beginning. As a teenager he designed experiments at Burnaby Lake to see if a red-winged blackbird's wing-patch size affected breeding success. He also trapped and banded finches in his backyard, assuming that just one small flock foraged there; by the end of that same year, he'd banded 1,100 finches. Later, he landed seasonal work as a naturalist with BC Parks and, in 1969, became curator of the University of BC's Cowan Vertebrate Museum. In 1973, still working on his bachelor's degree from the University of Victoria, he beat out six candidates with advanced credentials to win the job of curator of ornithology at Victoria's Royal British Columbia Museum, a position he would occupy for twenty years and where he truly made his mark.

"I'm the only employee in the history of the provincial government who has spent a minimum of a hundred days a year in the field," he claims. "My best year was 207 days. It was so important to be out there." During those years, besides earning a master's degree from the University of Washington in his spare time, Campbell conducted hundreds of wildlife inventories in remote corners of the province, visiting offshore islands to build a census of seabird breeding colonies. This research led to the establishment of Canada's first ecological reserves, including eight-hectare Cleland Island off Tofino, which teems with murres and cormorants. "Now," he says, "85 percent of all the seabird colonies in BC are protected." In 1992, he was appointed to the Order of British Columbia for his pioneering work on seabird conservation.

Throughout his years with the museum Campbell travelled extensively to speak to wildlife groups, impressing on birders in nearly every community in BC the invaluable contributions to scientific knowledge that even one amateur naturalist can make. This collaborative approach to gathering data culminated in the groundbreaking *Birds of British Columbia,* with its comprehensive observations on bird distribution and breeding locations by 5,000 reporters. Poet and fellow bird enthusiast Robert Bringhurst has called it "the basic work of reference to the land in which I live." No other bird book in Canada comes close to providing this degree of detail.

Upon leaving the museum in 1993 Campbell worked as a senior research scientist at the wildlife branch of BC's Ministry of Environment, Lands and Parks. In 2003, he retired—if that word can be applied to anyone as active as Wayne Campbell—and devoted his energies fully to the development of a wildlife data centre, something he had long seen a need for. This facility, a central repository for information about regional flora and fauna, would be the first of its kind in North America and perhaps the entire world.

Enter the Wild Bird Trust of BC (WBT). "We were approached by Wayne back in 1996 with this visionary concept of a data centre," says Patricia Banning-Lover. As I interview the silver-haired trust president, she is also searching for a press release, preparing for a photo shoot and instructing volunteers at Maplewood Flats, the trust's flagship bird sanctuary in North Vancouver. This is typical; her job description lists thirty-seven responsibilities, everything from government liaison to secretarial duties. Yet Banning-Lover receives nothing for the sixty to eighty-five hours she puts in each week. She is a volunteer, too.

"The thing with visionary concepts," she says, "is that they have to be translated into practical reality. But I love making things work." Wayne Campbell, who had seen WBT directors out clearing debris in their gumboots, was impressed by the organization's hands-on approach. The WBT folk, in turn, were excited by his experience and breadth of knowledge. It was a perfect match, though years of planning would still be required before the data centre could get off the ground.

The WBT president has her own visionary concept: that everyone who cares about birds joins a reputable natural history group, especially one that is actively working to preserve wildlife habitat. "A lot of people these days don't have time to volunteer," she says, "but they do have time to join. Your dues can help an organization accomplish more. If you have a couple of hours a week to volunteer, that's even better; there's a lot of work to be done."

Banning-Lover founded Wild Bird Trust in 1993 with her husband, Dr. Richard Beard, "to make BC a safer place for birds." Maplewood, the last undeveloped waterfront wetland on the north shore of Burrard Inlet, was the trust's first major project. Today this thirty-hectare former industrial zone is managed by Environment Canada while WBT operates the site as a conservation preserve.

Over the past decade, volunteers have transformed the degraded landscape into a "living classroom" and haven for wildlife. Banning-Lover leads me on a short tour along wheelchair-accessible trails that meander through a healthy forest of cottonwood and alder. Mud flats, a vital salt marsh and an interconnecting system of freshwater ponds and streams (designed by landscape architect Patrick Mooney) attract 229 species of birds, including a colony of rare purple martins. WBT members and the general public enjoy monthly nature walks with renowned naturalist Al Grass and numerous other community events, including the popular

Return of the Osprey Festival, a day of illustrated bird lectures, displays and guided strolls with local experts, held every July.

With the success of Maplewood, WBT went on to secure four more refuges: McFadden Creek on Saltspring Island, BC's largest breeding colony of great blue herons; Corrigan Nature Sanctuary, a small wooded location in Surrey with an education centre; thirty-three hectares of field and forest in Langley known as the Forslund Watson property; and, in 2002, Trincomali on Galiano Island, home to seabird colonies and peregrine falcons. Also in 2002, the organization purchased and renovated a Saanich building to serve as the long-anticipated Wild Bird Trust Wildlife Data Centre.

At WBT's Saanich data centre, Wayne Campbell and his thirty-three-year-old protege, Michael Preston, prepare to educate me about their latest activities. Their workplace, a modest split-level former house on Royal Oak Drive north of Campbell's Victoria home, is ideally located next to the private ponds and gardens of the 4.5-hectare Shangri-la Nature Sanctuary. Both men are thrilled to be working with Wild Bird Trust. "I was so impressed," says Campbell, "with how they tackled one project, followed through and then moved on to the next one."

The data centre, he explains, provides one-stop shopping for accurate, comprehensive, up-to-date information on BC wildlife. It has the largest bird library in the province. Mammals are well represented, too, as are reptiles, amphibians and even insects. Records of 4.5 million individual field observations are already stored in digital format, with 2,000 new ones added daily from more than 700 contributors around BC. The centre, he emphasizes, is designed for eventual self-sufficiency (corporate and institutional researchers will have to pay their way) and is already processing more than 200 information requests per month, mostly from BC.

Tall, earnest Mike Preston, English-born and Calgary-raised, is the centre's manager and a passionate researcher who designed its complex computer programs for storing and sorting data. In the foyer, Preston points out the Giving Wildlife a Chance Wall, though it's hard to miss: it's covered with plaques recognizing WBT volunteers. Here are tributes to sponsors such as Weyerhaeuser and the Australian vineyard and nature reserve Banrock Station, which has given the centre more than $36,000. A series of popular field guides, Campbell chips in, is another essential component of WBT's self-sufficiency vision: books on regional birds and birds in peril, to be co-published with Edmonton's Lone Pine Publishing, are already in the works.

The library, equipped with 340 metres of rolling shelves, houses an awesome collection of books, journals, manuscripts, theses, diaries and reports. Here is Campbell's personal trove of 65,000 bird articles and a vast array of original and photocopied field notes containing more than 10 million observations, all donated by local naturalists (such as Tony Greenfield on the Sunshine Coast, for instance). Upstairs are more files: on bird colonies, rare bird sightings and BC's Nest Records Scheme (120,000 "nest cards" detailing the breeding chronologies of provincial birds). Researchers also have access to some 100,000 bird photos.

Campbell had explained earlier how the library's nest records have been used by highway managers in the province to figure out when *not* to wash cliff swallow nests off bridges. The records, he says, could also be used to help control watercraft activity around nesting waterfowl. Now, seated behind a huge computer in his bookshelf-lined office, Preston tells the story of Creston naturalist Linda Van Damme, who recently became concerned about brush trimming along dikes in her area. Some shrubs, she knew, provided crucial habitat for nesting yellow warblers. So she contacted the data centre and Preston communed with his database. With a tap on the keyboard, he brings up a map showing yellow warbler abundance in BC. The dikes in question, it turns out, harbour far more of these birds than anywhere else in the province. Van Damme used this information to persuade the trimmers to back off. The warblers were saved.

With more taps, Preston's screen lays out other scenarios: how common loons cluster in certain areas off coastal BC at certain times of the year and could suffer a major disaster in an oil spill; how the spread across BC since 1889 of parasitic brown-headed cowbirds, which lay eggs in other birds' nests, raises concerns about their impact on island ecosystems; how western screech owls are being forced from their homes by urbanization, not by an expanding population of barred owls as biologists originally surmised. Campbell and Preston can use their data to correct assumptions, focus enquiries and pinpoint future concerns—all possible because of painstaking records kept by amateur BC naturalists. Sometimes, of course, the facts clash with conventional wisdom, annoying bureaucrats, business executives and environmentalists in equal measure. How does the centre maintain its independence? "It's easy," says Campbell. "We just show people the data. We don't interpret it—people can think. Give them the data and let them make their own decisions."

As well as showing folk the data, though, Campbell and Preston are also coming up with practical, research-based suggestions for everyday use by naturalists. They have determined, for instance, that BC's hummingbirds should be fed a mixture that is 50 percent sugar, not 25 percent, as the California-based feeder manufacturers often recommend. "Also, the colour of the feeder doesn't mean a thing," says Campbell.

Another discovery at the centre involves one of the biggest problems for birds, after habitat loss: windows, which kill hundreds of millions of birds a year in North America. According to Campbell, window decals don't help; what's really needed is for office towers to turn off their lights at night. The good news is that most birds don't break their necks on impact. "If you take that bird," he says, "hold it cupped loosely in your hands for two minutes then put it on a perch, 50 percent will live." And cats? The centre's data suggests a collar bell will reduce by 77 percent the number of birds a cat kills each year. Should you feed birds in summer? Sure, feed them all you want, says Campbell, just make sure the feeder is clean. Bacteria spread by bird feces are the killers, not too much food. "This is how we reach people," says Campbell. "We take the research, synthesize it, make it applicable, make it available and bring people closer to the work we're doing."

Sadly, in 2004 I hear that Campbell is ill and has found it necessary to take a year-long break from his work at the Wildlife Data Centre. Even more unhappily, WBT decides that it cannot afford to fund the facility in his absence and that the centre must be closed down. The library and files are returned to the Campbell residence until the dream can be resurrected.

But the closure of the centre in no way diminishes the importance of Campbell's vision or the enormous contribution he has made to protect wildlife and popularize conservation. "There's no better time than now," he says, "to work together to ensure that birds will have enough food, shelter and living space in the future." While more and more of us are seeing that biodiversity and ecosystem health are fundamental to the future, he knows that many wildlife lovers are motivated by intangible values, not data, and just want to know that wildlife is out there, that it exists and survives. But that's what Wayne Campbell is counting on. He may not be magician enough to turn barnyard turkeys into blue grouse, but his efforts are transforming the fate of BC's birds.

SAKINAW LAKE EMPTIES INTO THE OCEAN VIA A SHORT OUTLET STREAM.

Sakinaw Sockeye

Rare salmon in a Sunshine Coast lake

It's not difficult to see why so many affluent urbanites have built summer retreats beside the clear waters of Sakinaw Lake. Nine kilometres long, only eighty kilometres northwest of Vancouver, Sakinaw has a startling beauty, with richly forested hillsides and, in some areas, million-dollar views of the Coast Range. In July and August these waters buzz with powerboats and waterskiers, but in springtime, as I point my kayak round the lake's thirty-five-kilometre periphery, the place is silent and calm.

The main boat launch, just off Highway 101, is my put-in. A cheerful stream burbles into the lake just a few metres to the left, forming an apron of silt and sand that fans out along the shoreline. It's underwater beaches like this one—five of them, in particular—that have, in years gone by, attracted an unusual strain of small sockeye salmon to nest and lay its eggs. Unlike other salmon, this fish does not breed in the moving waters of stream or river, and it has unique genetic and biological features. Its numbers have dwindled drastically, and in 2002 it was designated as endangered by the federal Committee on the Status of Endangered Wildlife in Canada (COSEWIC). As a Sunshine Coast resident, I've heard a lot about the Sakinaw, the last remaining race of sockeye to breed round the shores of the Strait of Georgia. Now I want to see its home.

In 2004, at least, there were still a handful of salmon. Whether adult sockeye will return to the lake in future, though, is anybody's guess. The term "impending extinction" is in the air; alarm bells have finally gone off in Ottawa and Victoria. Grant McBain, community advisor in the Sunshine Coast area for Fisheries and Oceans Canada (FOC), predicts the run will survive.

As I work my way around the edge of the lake I enjoy the spring flowers—common red paintbrush, Pacific bleeding heart, saskatoon and yellow monkey-flower—that have gained rootholds on the cliffs. Soon I pass out of Sakinaw's small, shallow upper basin and paddle through a long neck into the lower basin, which is deeper and much larger. I marvel at the summer homes, many of which would not look out of place in West Vancouver. Some have fancy, terraced gardens and expansive lawns. Do they irrigate with lake water, I wonder. Do fertilizers and pesticides leach into these waters, another hurdle for the beleaguered fish?

Attempts to transplant alien sockeye to Sakinaw, or Sakinaw sockeye to other lakes, have failed. The population has collapsed mainly because a disproportionate number of Sakinaw fish end up in the nets of commercial fisheries that are targeting other stocks of salmon. But the lake's spawning beaches have also been degraded by logging activity over the years. Streams have been diverted. Lakeside habitat is affected by construction. The boat ramp where I put in was punched right through the middle of one prime beach site. Water usage affects water levels, as does climate, of course. Flows are sometimes too low for spawning adults to enter the lake. Further damage to the beaches, accidental or otherwise, and the demise of the sockeye could be rapid indeed.

The lake has numerous islands. Some are large and privately owned, with handsome cottages. Many others, though, are islets. There are tiny campsites on several, I hear. After two hours I come to a group of likely candidates and find a flat spot just big enough for a tent, with privacy and a view of the setting sun. A fat western painted turtle catches some final rays on a nearby log. Two common loons in breeding plumage make mournful calls as I cook dinner, and several beaver swim back and forth. Whenever they notice me they slap the water in alarm with their tails, then dive out of sight, only to return a few minutes later as if nothing had happened. As night falls, I burrow into a down sleeping bag, don a headlamp and continue my salmon studies.

Everyone loves the sleek, delicious sockeye, BC's most commercially valuable fish, with its silvery sides and metallic blue back. At spawning time the adults, especially the males, turn bright red, with olive green heads. Mature males develop humps and hooked jaws. Juveniles usually grow in "nursery" lakes. Because most lakes are geographically isolated and vary hugely in biological and physical terms, the salmon that adapt to them over the millennia often evolve in remarkable ways. The most distinct races are known to scientists as "nationally significant populations" or, in the US, as "evolutionarily significant units (ESUs)." For instance, seven aquatic zones with sockeye ESUs have been identified in the US. Two have been listed under the US Endangered Species Act as either threatened (Ozette Lake) or endangered (Snake River).

In Canada, most sockeye travel up the Fraser and Skeena rivers to spawn, and juveniles begin life in interior lakes. While there are many sockeye populations in Canada that would likely qualify as ESUs, only two—in Sakinaw Lake and Cultus Lake—are known, at present, to be in serious trouble. The Cultus sockeye, located in the Fraser Valley twelve kilometres south of Chilliwack and heavily affected by human activity, may be more endangered even than those from Sakinaw. As well as overfishing, Cultus sockeye must contend with lethal parasites, farm runoff and a heavy human recreational impact. The lake receives 1.5 million visitors annually and an enormous amount of pollution from power boats.

Then again, considering the actual population figures, it's difficult to imagine any race more desperate than the Sakinaw sockeye. Until 1987 fish returning to spawn in the lake numbered, on average, about 5,000 a year, with a peak of 16,000 in 1975. Since then, the totals have dropped steadily. By 1992 that average was close to 1,000; by 1996 it had dropped below 200; and by 2002 it was less than 50. In 2003, despite a thorough count, only three spawning fish—one male and two females—were seen.

Next morning after breakfast, I pack up and paddle to the end of the lake, where a floating walkway prevents wood debris from blocking the exit and leads to a trail to the sea. Sakinaw, which has an elevation of only five metres, drains into Georgia Strait via a short stream. At the outlet there's a small dam, where water levels are controlled and adult salmon

LOOKING NORTHEAST ON SAKINAW FROM THE LAKE'S OUTLET

must enter the lake via a fishway. A crew of three fisheries technicians is working there, counting smolts. (Salmon are called smolts when they first set off to sea.) A few young sockeye, at least, are leaving their birthplace, beginning their perilous journey through Georgia and Johnstone straits to the North Pacific, where they will spend two summers before returning to Sakinaw by the same route. Then the adult salmon will spend an unusual length of time (up to six months) in the seven-square-kilometre lake before spawning in late November.

At the dam I run into FOC's Grant McBain, who is supervising the salmon counters. The departing smolts pass over the dam and are diverted to a holding tank. Sockeye is not the only species the crew finds; coho salmon and sea-run cutthroat trout also inhabit Sakinaw and its tributaries. McBain points out the remains of an old dam. In the early 1900s, he says, loggers boomed their logs on the lake and blocked the outlet. Then, when the water level rose, they shot logs through to the sea, a practice that scoured the outflow stream and damaged fish habitat at either end. In 1952 the federal government built a permanent dam and fishway, and lake levels are now regulated for the benefit of both sockeye and Sakinaw residents.

Huge logs from the early days still lurk beneath the lake's surface. The wood is quite usable, preserved perfectly by the meromictic, or permanently stratified, waters; similar century-old saturated logs have been salvaged from adjacent Ruby Lake. Salvage operations in Sakinaw, though, could further damage the sockeye's spawning grounds. Meromictic lakes are quite rare; only a dozen or so exist in all Canada and less than a dozen in the US. In Sakinaw, a thirty-metre layer of fresh water lies over a warmer layer that is anoxic, or lacking in oxygen, and dense with dissolved mineral salts. In normal lakes, oxygen-rich surface waters cool in autumn and sink, thus displacing and oxygenating deeper waters. In a meromictic lake, the layers are prevented from mixing because of the lower level's unusually high density. In fact, Sakinaw's two layers may not have mixed in thousands of years.

The area around the lake's outlet is a Sechelt First Nation reserve, and many of the technicians employed locally are Sechelt members. The Sakinaw sockeye was once a significant food source for the Sechelt people, and they are intensely interested in any attempts to restore the depleted stock. In fact, the actual word sockeye—or *stsek̲ay*, with its hissing pronunciation—comes directly from *shashishahlem*, the Sechelt language. A series of ancient red ochre pictographs with columns of fish and marine mammal shapes mark a sheer rock face on the lake's north shore. Several sockeye runs used to exist in Sechelt territory, but Sakinaw was always the most important. "There were rock fish weirs at the mouth at one time," says Jerry Johnson, senior fisheries technician for the Sechelt First Nation, "but the loggers destroyed them." The weirs were constructed in such a way that the sockeye were diverted to holding pools; when the tide went out the fish could be harvested on the beach.

Johnson is a member of the Sakinaw Lake Sockeye Recovery Team, a group of specialists formed by FOC in 2003 to reverse the fish's decline. The team includes biologists and fisheries managers, commercial and sport fishers, property owners, planners and conservationists. According to McBain, in addition to the work of the recovery team, FOC will try to ensure that BC's numerous fisheries catch no more than 12 percent of adult Sakinaw sockeye. Work will be undertaken to restore spawning habitat, improve the fishway so that adult salmon can re-enter the lake without trouble, and monitor predators (otters and seals) at the outlet. Human impacts on the lake will be studied, as will water-level issues and marine survival rates for adult sockeye. "I think we've caught it just in time," he says of the struggle to revive the fish.

McBain also tells me about the hatchery program that, for the past four years, has raised Sakinaw salmon fry in order to enhance the lake's sockeye population. In 2004 the first hatchery adults were expected back at the lake to help boost the number of spawners. And indeed, in mid-July 2004 when I touch base by phone, he tells me that five adult fish have returned, two more than in all of 2003, with the run yet to peak. A related fisheries program raises Sakinaw sockeye for broodstock, but as recovery team member Dr. John Field, a

DEPARTING SMOLTS AND RETURNING ADULT SALMON ARE COUNTED AT THE SAKINAW DAM.

Capilano College biology instructor and local conservationist, notes, this is really "a last resort. It's like having the fish in a zoo situation, where they're kept and bred in captivity in case the wild fish completely disappear."

Field, a director of the Sunshine Coast Conservation Association, is convinced that his organization brings a vital, much-needed perspective to the recovery team. "One of our goals," he says, "is to consider the wider ecosystem, to view the needs of the salmon in a broader environmental context. Another goal is to make sure that the public has a stake in the recovery process and is kept well-advised. For the process to be successful in the long term and for the sockeye to return to health, it's the public, including the users of Sakinaw Lake and those who live round its shores, who must really take ownership of the plan."

On my return paddle, as I work my way around the rest of Sakinaw's shoreline, I consider the larger ecosystem. A trail leads off to Kokomo Lake, but I can't find it. Everything is overgrown. At the north end of Sakinaw a large stream, choked with vegetation, leads to Ruby Lake, which has its own miniature constellation of lakes, including Ambrose, made an ecological reserve in 1971 to protect a perfect, unspoiled specimen of a coastal bog lake. The day before, on the south side of Sakinaw, I'd passed the entrance stream for another little system of lakes: Mixal, which has a coho run, and the linked chain of Katherine, Garden Bay and Hotel lakes. The complexity of water issues in this one small region is boggling.

A few weeks after my visit I'm forcefully reminded of it. Federal fisheries minister Geoff Regan announces a nine-month delay before deciding whether to list twelve endangered aquatic species, including the Sakinaw salmon, under the Species at Risk Act. Regan also rejects a call for emergency protection of the salmon under the act. Elizabeth May, executive director of the Sierra Club of Canada, calls the rejection "an extinction order for the sockeye salmon of Sakinaw and Cultus lakes." On the ground, though, the work of the Sakinaw recovery team continues. By early September, ninety-nine fish had returned to the lake. As long as a handful of salmon remain, it seems that a few dedicated individuals will keep trying to protect them.

GARRY OAKS IN WINTER AT OAK BAY'S UPLANDS PARK

Quercus Garryana

The troubled ecosystem of BC's only oak

Walking through Victoria's Beacon Hill Park one winter, admiring the 400-year-old groves of Garry oak, I stooped to pick up a couple of acorns and slip them into my pocket. Over the next few weeks, these acorns, fruit of BC's only oak species, found their way to my dresser, then to the kitchen, and finally to a planter outside our Sunshine Coast home. There I promptly forgot about them.

At the time, I knew little about the Garry oak, or *Quercus garryana*. I was vaguely aware that it wasn't doing too well. Stately and craggy-limbed, the tree towers over the same warm, dry, south-facing slopes we covet for shopping centres and homes. In BC it only occurs on the Gulf Islands, on southeastern Vancouver Island and at a few other isolated locations. Over the last two centuries, more than 95 percent of oak woodlands and meadows have been lost to development or severely damaged by invasive species. For the past thirteen years, the Garry Oak Meadow Preservation Society (*www.garryoak.bc.ca*) has been trying to reverse this destruction.

Twenty different oak species grow on the west coast of North America, with the Garry oak having the widest distribution, from BC to California. To the south, it is vital habitat for acorn woodpeckers and is commonly known as Oregon white oak. It is preferred for foraging and nesting by a host of birds, including raptors. The acorns are eaten by deer, bear and rodents, and were gathered by First Nations groups, especially in California, and ground into meal. The wood is prized for fuel, and has, in the past, been used for everything from pallets to ships. Today it is harvested in small quantities for Oregon craftsmen to make specialty wine barrels. Saltspring Island's Garry Oaks Winery ages its pinot noir in them, claiming they're the next best thing to French oak for flavour.

With its extensive root system, the Garry oak helps stabilize steep watershed slopes and has been employed in the restoration of ravaged grassland habitats. In urban areas, it's a highly valued ornamental. Even south of the border, though, this once-flourishing species is in decline throughout its range. The tree is vulnerable to destructive fungi, such as white pocket and shoestring root rots. And conifer seedlings, controlled in the old days by frequent but minor grass fires, are steadily invading the oak meadows now that fire is routinely suppressed.

If undisturbed, Garry oak forms a distinctive, open, parklike habitat, sometimes referred to as a savannah. Captain George Vancouver, a hard man to please, found the oak landscapes of southern Vancouver Island "as enchantingly beautiful as the most elegantly finished pleasure ground in Europe." This was in the late 1700s. Seventy years later, those wooded surroundings reminded Victoria's first settlers of their British homeland, and they, too, raved about the domesticated appearance of the countryside. Under the trees, an array of delicate plants—satin-flower, chocolate lily, shooting star, sea blush—blossomed each spring in scented waves of purple, blue, pink, white and gold. These meadows had, in fact, been cultivated with great care for centuries by the region's Songhees and Esquimalt inhabitants, who prized as food the camas bulbs that grew there in profusion.

BC's Conservation Data Centre considers that ninety-one of the species making up the Garry oak ecosystems are at risk provincially. The Committee on the Status of Endangered Wildlife in Canada (COSEWIC) lists twenty-one of these species threatened at the national level, including twelve—one moss, eight vascular plants, two butterflies and the sharp-tailed snake—classified as endangered, the highest level of concern. A scarce BC bird, Lewis's woodpecker, has already disappeared from its coastal oak habitats, though it survives in the interior. While the oak trees themselves are fairly plentiful, the communities of plants and animals they anchor are the rarest in the province. Most, in fact, are balanced on the knife-edge of extinction.

These communities are the most diverse terrestrial ecosystems in BC, harbouring at least 694 plant species. Twenty percent of the province's rarest plants grow nowhere else. The communities are distinguished mainly by plant composition; the two main types are the "parkland" ecosystems that occupy deeper, richer soils and the "scrub" systems that cling to rocky outcrops. Another reason for keeping these plant communities healthy is that they may have an essential role to play if global warming persists. Because they are well adapted to warmth and summer droughts, Garry oak ecosystems can take over from retreating Douglas fir in many areas. Over the millenia Douglas fir and Garry oak likely engaged in a see-saw battle for dominance in southern BC. The jostling continues.

Indeed, back on the Sunshine Coast, my acorns decided to join the fray. Much to my surprise, first one sprouted, then the other. I transplanted them to pots and watched their silken leaves unfold and search out the sun. The seedlings seemed to take a liking to their new home, and I grew strangely fond of these brave immigrants in alien territory. True, small colonies of Garry oak survive in several unlikely spots, including Savary Island and Yale, but none, as far as I know, exist in my specific part of the world.

The tree is not difficult to grow, I discovered. You need intact, robust acorns, and should probably plant several, as all may not germinate. Half-metre sections of ten-centimetre plastic drain pipe make ideal containers for seedlings, as a long taproot is the first thing to sprout. Keep the soil moist but not wet. When replanting, consider that Garry oaks are intolerant of shade and saplings may need protection from browsing animals. The trees grow slowly but ultimately become huge, so they should be sited with care.

As my interest in the species grew, I searched out prime oak habitat on visits to Victoria, and gradually became familiar with Mount Tolmie, Gonzales Hill, Mill Hill, Bear Hill, Lone Tree Hill, Horth Hill and other ridge-top parks, all of which have lovely oak woodlands. Christmas Hill, its rock faces upholstered with licorice fern, is a particular delight. At Uplands Park in Oak Bay, a fine example of the rare "valley bottom" oak ecosystem can be enjoyed. Throughout the Capital Regional District I was encouraged to see volunteer groups and parks employees at work among the oaks eradicating Scotch broom and reintroducing the threatened plant species.

THE THICK, CRACKED BARK OF AN ANCIENT GARRY OAK

To view a more intensive restoration project, I travelled to Maple Bay near Duncan, where, in 1999, the Nature Conservancy of Canada had acquired an eleven-hectare former dairy farm, the best unprotected oak habitat remaining at that time. There I interrupted Irvin Banman, who was weeding trays of spring-gold and Hooker's onion seedlings with a pair of tweezers, and he kindly walked me around the renamed Cowichan Garry Oak Preserve.

Winter among the oaks, while not as dramatic as spring, has its own stark beauty. A dense, continuous stand of leafless, moss-and-lichen-covered trees occupies half the site, which is also home to endangered golden Indian paintbrush, Howell's triteleia, white-top aster, deltoid balsamroot and yellow montane violet. Banman steered us away from these red-listed rarities while describing efforts being made to remove exotic plants, restock native ones and return the ecosystem to its original state. Before leaving, we paid our respects to some veteran oaks, including one giant with a trunk over five metres in circumference, believed to be the largest surviving example of its race in BC.

Today, one of the few benefits of being endangered is that, because of the federal Species at Risk Act (SARA), a recovery team may be speeding its way to assist you. Teams are sprouting up everywhere, for all kinds of flora and fauna, and the Garry Oak Ecosystems Recovery Team, or GOERT (*www.goert.ca*), already has a short-term plan for minimizing further habitat loss and motivating future protection activities. In the long term, with strong support evinced by the region's local governments, the team hopes to establish a network of oak ecosystems sufficient to improve the health of the endangered plants and get them off COSEWIC's list.

The immediate effort, or Phase I, is scheduled to last five years and include the gathering of scientific information necessary to get a broader recovery program going, preventing any more damage to existing sites and encouraging preservation and stewardship activities with public education programs. Phase II, to begin in 2006, would involve the acquisition and restoration of additional properties with oak ecosystems.

In Halfmoon Bay, meanwhile, our saplings thrive. We've christened them Quercus and Garryana. (This species of oak, incidentally, was named by intrepid nineteenth-century botanist David Douglas in honour of Nicholas Garry, a deputy governor of the Hudson's Bay Company.) Quercus, squat and gnarly, seems to grow mostly sideways, but glorious Garryana, after five years, is over two metres tall. They occupy a couple of expensive half barrels and are overdue for transfer to permanent locations. I'm hoping that, with a little bit of luck, they're here to stay.

Most of my paddling takes place, naturally enough, in the region round my home. The Sunshine Coast is just a ferry ride northwest of Greater Vancouver, and I'm fortunate to have a world of maritime opportunities at my doorstep. Katherine Johnston, my partner, is also a keen paddler, and together we've subjected our local inlets and sounds to a fair degree of scrutiny. Many of the chapters that follow detail these journeys and, I hope, offer proof that you don't have to go far from the city in BC to have a wilderness kayaking experience.

Other kayaking chapters, both in this section and elsewhere in the book, take us farther afield, to the Gulf Islands, the shores of Vancouver Island, the central coast, Haida Gwaii and the Discovery Islands at the northern end of Georgia Strait. Many of the chapters in the final section, "Islands Everywhere," have paddling themes, as do parts of the "Sakinaw Sockeye" and "Cortes Culture" chapters. We were joined on several expeditions by our friends Elaine Futterman and Mike Allegretti, whom you will meet shortly if you read on. We thank them for their gracious company, paddling smarts and outdoor culinary skills, and hope they'll still want to kayak with us after they've seen this book.

Kayaking Tales

ON THE CURME ISLANDS IN DESOLATION SOUND

Desolation Sound

From Okeover Arm to the Curme Islands

A fine wilderness campsite, used with care and respect by visitors over many years, can be a place of almost archaeological beauty. Our perch in the Curme Islands, with its grandstand view of Desolation Sound Provincial Marine Park, is a case in point. There's a flat area for a tent, of course, but also a log table and chairs, and a firepit with a grill. An elegant chess and checkers board has been inscribed into the rough table top. Across the water an intricate network of coves, channels, beaches and headlands awaits leisurely exploration by kayak. For now, we stretch out and relax.

The site's ultimate touch, to me, is the artful stone staircase that leads down to the tideline and looks, at first glance, like a natural formation. My eternal gratitude goes out to whoever built this. The part about kayaking that will probably kill me in the end is carrying the darned boats up and down steep rocky shorelines slick with seaweed and booby-trapped with razor-sharp barnacles. But here we have a set of steps. I feel as if I've stumbled across an entrance to an abandoned village from some ancient maritime civilization.

As a location for playing Robinson Crusoe, the Curme Islands cannot be eclipsed. Rufous hummingbirds practise their dive-bomb techniques while Douglas squirrels lecture us from the trees. Fat garter snakes laze in the sun. Gnarled manzanitas, all grey-green leaves and writhing red limbs, rise above a thick underbrush of salal, juniper and kinnikinnick. Below our camp the tide retreats to reveal a series of lagoons, warm enough for a quick dip, where rock crabs scurry and multi-hued bat stars patrol the eelgrass.

Were we here in midsummer, we'd no doubt have to share our island kingdom with other paddlers. But this week, a scorcher in the shoulder season, we're undisturbed. A canoeing couple has taken over the islet to the north. South of us, eight kayakers lay claim to a third island and find sufficient tentsites amid the scattered outcrops of Douglas-fir, shore pine and arbutus. The fourth member of the Curme group, steep-sided and inhospitable, remains home, as far as we can tell, only to kingfishers and a pair of bald eagles.

This is our first foray into BC's largest marine park. Katherine and I have prepared by quizzing our Roberts Creek friends Elaine Futterman and Mike Allegretti about the area, poring over maps after dinner, marking possible campsites and hearing their stories. Mike has just retired from teaching high-school science; Elaine is a marine biologist turned potter; together they operate Creek Clayworks and craft a popular line of sumptuous, richly glazed tablewares. Over two decades they have made more than a dozen extended trips in their double kayak through Desolation Sound and beyond, and they've got us excited about exploring these complex waterways.

"The sound is relatively calm," says Elaine, "with swimmable water and beautiful scenery. Crossings are manageable, which is good if you're a bit of a chicken. And you can even get cappuccinos at Refuge Cove. But it can also be a challenging place to paddle. We've been stormed out of there. We had to abort an entire trip because the weather was so bad and the waves so high."

"It's fairly easy paddling," adds Mike. "As you head more to the east, into Homfray Channel, it goes from being a nice, sedate area to very rugged, with big mountains. I would say it's my favourite place for a 'holiday' paddle, as opposed to an 'adventure' paddle."

Mike and Elaine have seen more and more kayakers in Desolation Sound since the paddling guidebooks started focusing on the area. Large touring groups are overburdening some of the more intimate camping spots. All heavily used sites need to be equipped with toilets, they suggest.

Katherine and I put in at Okeover Arm Provincial Park, near the terminus of Highway 101 at Lund. It's a three-hour paddle to Desolation Sound, but we manage to catch a ride with a northward-flowing current—easy to do between May and September when daytime tides are usually low. Parklands surround us as we float along: to the right, Gifford Peninsula, part of the 8,449-hectare Desolation Sound park; to the left, newly established Malaspina Provincial Park. Boaters can go ashore nearly anywhere, except at a few private holdings decked out with summer homes.

There are all kinds of coves to explore and side trips to take without even leaving these protected waters. Lancelot Inlet, for instance, leads off to our right and ends in Wootton Bay.

Another inlet, Theodosia, branches eastward from Lancelot. South of the entrance to Theodosia is Thynne Island, where naturalist Archibald Menzies and a boat crew from Captain George Vancouver's HMS *Discovery* had breakfast on June 27, 1792, after determining that Theodosia, sadly, did not lead to the fabled Northwest Passage.

In fact, the shallow inlet terminates in extensive mudflats and a broad grassy estuary, site of a Sliammon First Nation reserve named Toquana. Until the 1920s, the Sliammon people occupied a village there with houses built on stilts to avoid annual flooding. Later on, Theodosia became a major log-booming area. There's a forestry road I'd like to hike sometime that leads from the inlet to Powell Lake, passing by the abandoned farming community of Foch at Olsen Lake.

Grace Harbour, just north of the entrance to Lancelot, makes another excellent detour. Grace has the feel of a haven; it's a complete sanctuary from waves and weather. Another First Nation reserve, Kah Kay Kay, is located on the northern shore. This was once an important winter village not only for the Sliammon but also for the Klahoose and Homalco people, whose traditional territories are farther north. All three groups shared the site and it was occupied into the 1960s. At the head of the harbour a trail leads to marshy meadows and a beaver-dammed lake.

By the time we finally exit Malaspina Inlet and round Zephine Head, the mid-morning breeze has disappeared. Desolation Sound is about as calm as it ever gets. Instead of investigating nearby Galley Bay as we'd planned, we head straight across the sound to the Curme Islands, another hour's work. The view takes our minds off the effort of paddling; the northeastern horizon is filled with jagged, snowy peaks, dominated by Mount Addenbroke on East Redonda

PADDLING PRIDEAUX HAVEN IN DESOLATION SOUND
WITH MOUNT DENMAN AS A BACKDROP

Island—at 1,600 metres the highest peak in BC on an island other than Vancouver Island—and the 2,000-metre horn of Mount Denman.

Despite the Curmes' attractions, the rest of Desolation Sound also beckons. In the mornings we cruise over to Prideaux Haven and Tenedos Bay, famed anchorages for recreational mariners. We enter Prideaux by its back door, a narrow passage between the mainland and Eveleigh Island, too shallow for regular craft. Although there are few boats present at this time of year, the drone of diesel engines still floats across the water. Gotta keep the shower water hot, the icemaker cold and the satellite dish correctly tuned.

To the east the haven becomes a labyrinth of tiny waterways, jutting rocks and kelp-jungle tidepools—perfect for kayakers. Two small coves, named Melanie and Laura, preserve traces of old homesteads where exotic plants linger on overgrown rock terraces. Common mergansers and murres seem unaffected by our presence, while black oystercatchers screech at us to keep our distance. With the Unwin Range soaring overhead and a rich mantle of vegetation covering all surfaces, this is one of the prettiest parts of the park.

It was around here that some of Captain Vancouver's crew members came across an infamous village of fleas. Vancouver, of course, was the one who bestowed upon this glorious region the name of Desolation Sound. Illness and depression had brought him low at this point in his journey. "Our residence here was truly forlorn," he wrote. "An awful silence pervaded the gloomy forests, whilst animated nature seemed to have deserted the neighbouring country." Anchored for several weeks in Lewis Channel at the entrance to Teakerne Arm, he mapped the area using ship's boats, one of which was commanded by Archibald Menzies.

Menzies and his men came across a deserted village "placed on the summit of an elevated projecting rock." It was home, Menzies estimated, to as many as 300 people in winter. Unfortunately, in summer the village "swarmed with a myriad of fleas," and he and his party "were obliged to quit the rock in great precipitation." The sailors stripped off their clothes and threw themselves in the ocean, but the fleas "leaped about as frisky as ever." They even towed the offending garments behind their boat. "In the evening we steeped them in boiling water," Menzies wrote.

Today's visitors encounter no such terrors. At Tenedos Bay, where visitors will find wooden tent platforms, toilets and a valuable source of fresh water, a short trail leads to Unwin Lake's log-choked exit point. You can swim here, in water that gets lukewarm in summer. As we depart the bay we glance at

Bold Head, at the entrace to Tenedos, and see the clear profile of a severe, rugged face—Desolation Sound's equivalent of Mount Rushmore or the Sphinx—keeping guard over the park.

When it's time to head home, we reluctantly point our bows along the north shore of Gifford Peninsula, passing Portage Cove, where the manicured fields of a private homestead occupy a narrow isthmus between Desolation Sound and Lancelot Inlet. Further west is Galley Bay, another private enclave, where a row of handsome summer homes belie the fact that here in the 1970s flourished one of BC's largest and best known counterculture communes. Its tradition of communal nudity (in summer) did not go unnoticed by recreational mariners anchored in the bay.

Rounding Zephine Head again, where paddlers must be wary of unruly waves, we pick up a flooding tide and southbound current and zip down Malaspina and Okeover inlets to our starting point. We've only managed to sample the high points of a spectacular region, and I suspect we'll soon be back.

A QUARTET OF CALIFORNIA SEA LIONS IN SECHELT INLET

Round Sechelt Inlet

An inland sea on Vancouver's doorstep

At the head of Narrows Inlet, where the estuary of the Tzoonie River meets saltwater, the mountains crowd in. This place was once the site of a Sechelt First Nation village, but there's a forestry camp there now, and steep, switchbacked logging roads have eroded many of the surrounding slopes. Even so, it's still very beautiful. Katherine and I paddle close to shore, over calm waters that mirror forest and sky. Beneath the surface thousands of small moon jellyfish gleam like pale lamps. We've noticed these translucent discs everywhere on our journey, but as we move toward the river's mouth, the drifts of jellies grow thicker and deeper. Countless galaxies of medusae are massing as far as we can see, turning the water white with their ghostly, pulsating flesh.

It's late August, and with our single kayaks we are exploring Sechelt Inlet, only sixty kilometres northwest of Vancouver.

This handy inland ocean is perched right on the city's back doorstep, though few urban dwellers take advantage of it. You need four or five days, at least, to get a sense of the area if you're paddling and a week or more if you want to see it all. The main inlet, which joins Jervis Inlet at its northern end, is thirty-five kilometres long; its two tributaries, Salmon Inlet and Narrows Inlet, branch off to the east, adding an additional twenty-three and fifteen kilometres, respectively. The mouth of the inlet is guarded by mighty Skookumchuck Rapids, a punishing bottleneck for boaters wishing to enter or exit. The rapids are BC's swiftest tidal flow, a boiling maelstrom of whirlpools and standing waves that can reach an astonishing sixteen knots, or almost thirty kilometres per hour.

We've decided to point our bows toward picturesque Tzoonie Narrows on Narrows Inlet. Although most kayakers drive to the residential suburb of Tuwanek on the east side of Sechelt Inlet to launch, we put in instead at Porpoise Bay in downtown Sechelt. This is the southern tip of the inlet and its shorelines are well populated; powerboats and float planes are frequent sights. We paddle along the less developed western side of the bay, and at Carlson Point pause to consider the predicament of a community of cabin owners, whose decades-long seclusion has been shattered by a very intrusive logging operation.

The mouth of Carlson Creek is a transition zone of sorts—a reminder, if you will, of a way of life that used to flourish in these parts. Here lies what's left of the home of the Solberg sisters, Bergliot and Minnie. Their parents, Herman and Olga Solberg, were Norwegian immigrants; Herman handlogged and trapped around Sechelt Inlet in the late 1920s and '30s. Bergie and Minnie carried on the family traditions, working until they were well into their seventies. Bergie, known as the

Cougar Lady, sold her raccoon and mink skins to buyers from Vancouver. The sisters supplied their own venison, and Bergie was noted for her singing, yodelling and guitar playing. With their hats and bush clothes, the pair were a familiar if unconventional sight in Sechelt, where they made occasional forays for supplies.

Several years ago Minnie became ill and had to be moved to a nursing home in Sechelt, where she died in 2001. Bergie refused to leave her ramshackle digs, which she shared with her dog Bush and four goats. "If I went into town," she said to her friend Jim Wilkinson, "I would die." In November 2002, after failing to respond to repeated calls on the CB radio that Wilkinson had set up for her, she was found on the floor of her cabin, dead of natural causes, with Bush by her side. Bergliot Solberg was eighty years old. On this part of the inlet, at least, a pioneer era had come to a close.

Beyond Carlson Creek, Katherine and I pause to explore the pleasant little recreation area on the south side of Piper Point, one of nine wilderness campsites located within provincial parks on the three inlets. North of here the landscape becomes wilder and far less populated. It takes us three leisurely hours to reach the larger campsite at Halfway Beach, also on the inlet's west shore. Osprey wheel overhead, keening like babies as we set up camp in an alder grove and gather wood for an evening beach fire.

Before cooking dinner we clamber over to a little rock promontory where the sun lingers long after Halfway Beach itself is in shadow. There are wonderful views here of Sechelt and Salmon inlets, and a strange, elevated lagoon that only gets flushed by very high tides. My eagle-eyed partner spots

LOOKING UP SECHELT INLET FROM HALFWAY BEACH
WITH HALFWAY ISLET IN THE MID-DISTANCE

what she thinks might be fish bones, and we crouch down to find the well-preserved skeleton of a harbour seal, picked clean by scavengers, in one corner of the pool.

In summer, strong thermal winds often develop by late morning and blow up Sechelt Inlet until late afternoon, so we rise early and try to do most of our paddling before eleven a.m. It's dead calm the next morning as we cross from Halfway Beach to Kunechin Point, a delightful peninsula formed where Salmon and Sechelt inlets join. En route we see plenty of live seals, mostly mothers with pups at this time of year. Kunechin, with its rocky headlands, coves and islands, is a glorious camping spot and also popular with sport divers. (The 110-metre HMCS *Chaudiere*, an obsolete destroyer escort, was sunk there in 1992 as an artificial reef. Attempts to deposit a defunct Boeing 737 jetliner as an additional lure for

THE CARETAKERS' CABIN AT CLOWHOM LAKE LODGE AT THE HEAD OF SALMON INLET

divers were scuttled by the Sechelt First Nation and local conservationists in 2003.)

Farther north, just before we enter Narrows Inlet, we paddle round the shoreline of Storm Bay, the safest anchorage in the region for boaters. A Vancouver company, Sechelt Brick and Tile, started a brickworks here in 1907, but the clay was of poor quality and the plant closed by 1909. After World War I, in order to employ returned soldiers, the works were started up again with federal funding, but the clay was as poor as before and the project soon foundered. Purloined bricks from Storm Bay have built many a fireplace and smokehouse on the Sunshine Coast.

In summer, Storm Bay is the site of a small but vibrant neighbourhood. There are unusual homes hidden away in the trees, a legacy of the bay's long existence as a counterculture commune. First settled in the late 1960s by Peter Light, the bay was later colonized by members of the Western Front, a Vancouver artists' co-operative. Many well-known experimental artists have found inspiration here, including Glenn Lewis, Hank Bull, videographer Kate Craig, filmmaker David Rimmer and others.

The isolated cottage communities on the three inlets, such as Carlson Point and Storm Bay, lead a tentative existence these days, subject as they are to the whims of the forest industry. Logging activity, which is extensive throughout the region, has touched both places in the past few years, and residents have had to mount vigorous campaigns to preserve their views and water sources. The BC government, through its own small-business program, has allowed logging contractors to cut right to the edge of the Carlson Point properties; in Storm Bay a flood of protest has persuaded Interfor to move harvesting boundaries out of the area. The inlets' priceless viewscapes, so essential to any future form of ecotourism, are supposedly protected through provincial legislation; the degree to which any particular view can be disturbed by cutting, however, is regularly altered and diluted by forestry bureaucrats in order to ensure a constant flow of logs.

As we proceed into Narrows Inlet those viewscapes change. Mountains rise up sharply on either side, with vertical bluffs and treeless cliffs—home to mountain goats. Considerable logging has taken place at lower elevations, but you hardly notice it because your eyes are constantly drawn upward. Tzoonie Narrows, with a tidal flow that peaks at four knots (a dribble compared to nearby Skookumchuck and only an impediment for a kayaker at maximum flood or ebb), is halfway along the inlet. There are old fruit trees and waterfront clearings just west of the narrows where pioneer homesteads and an Osborne Logging camp once stood.

Now the area is a provincial park, and today it's full of camping kayakers, here on an organized tour. Tzoonie can get crowded on summer weekends, but we find a patch of grass to pitch our tent just beyond tour-group central. At the edge of our campsite some old machinery—a huge donkey engine and winch, the tracks and chassis of an excavator—is rusting away like debris on a battlefield. At first these industrial castoffs offend me (why shouldn't logging companies be required to clean up after themselves?), but we grow to appreciate them; they make excellent cooking platforms. We see about twenty kayakers our first day at the narrows, but on the second day everyone leaves and we have the place to ourselves.

In the 1970s, while the Storm Bay community was in early bloom, Narrows Inlet also had a resident population. There was no park in those days. A group of young people squatted at the narrows, living in abandoned logging camp buildings, now long gone. Daniel Bouman, a Gibsons photographer and executive director of the Sunshine Coast Conservation Association, spent seven years at the narrows, from 1973 to 1980. He was a refugee from the US, a draft dodger, and he'd heard about the area from friends in Vancouver.

"After a couple of years in the camp I built an eight-sided, two-storey cabin on the opposite side of Narrows Inlet," Bouman recalls. He had a series of small boats, grew vegetables, caught seafood and went to Sechelt or Egmont once in a while for the few supplies he needed. Two months of tree-planting in springtime provided him with sufficient funds. "It was a rich social life, with everyone going back and forth across the inlet. We had CB radios and a network of people on the air every night." Excursions to Storm Bay and farther afield required overnight stays or longer. "And we were raided, of course, at regular intervals by RCMP and narcotics and immigration people, and even visited by Jehovah's Witnesses."

Bouman left the inlet eventually, to build boats in Sechelt. "I was a pretty young fella at the time, and I didn't really have any idea of what I wanted to do. But I went to Narrows Inlet and learned to rely on myself. I learned a lot of basic things: how to look after engines, how to construct boats and buildings, how to be on the water, how to feed myself. And I learned a lot of stuff the hard way about how to get along with people."

In many ways, the experiences of Bouman and his pals echo those of a previous generation of Sechelt Inlet back-to-the-landers. The inhabitants of Doriston, for instance, located just south of the Skookumchuck on the northeast shore of Sechelt Peninsula—and only reachable by boat or float plane—were learning similar "basic things" fifty years earlier. I've cruised past this tiny hamlet on a number of occasions, admiring the orchards and well-maintained gardens, the bulging woodpiles, the workmanlike sheds and boat ramps. Doriston may be only a shadow of its former self, but it's still inhabited; plumes of smoke rise from chimneys and friendly figures often wave. At one time, though, it was a typical BC coastal community: isolated, self-sufficient and seafaring.

Doriston got its start at the turn of the century with a sawmill built by Bert Whitaker, an entrepreneur who owned a series of stores and hotels in Sechelt. The first permanent resident was a man named Austin Shaw. Other settlers moved in, and they logged and fished and farmed. A school opened as early as 1912; there was a post office, named Shaw Cove, by 1915 and telegraph service by about 1920. Sam Lloyd arrived before World War I, and when Shaw went off to join the army, Lloyd became postmaster and renamed the community after his daughter Doris. As part of his duties, he rowed to Sechelt and back, a distance of fifty-five kilometres, once a week to fetch the mail.

The post office was closed by 1923, but the school lingered on until 1939. Enrollment normally varied between eight and twelve children. The teachers were dedicated souls; Hilda Cuttle, for instance, served at Doriston from 1930 to 1938, teaching all grades from one to twelve, giving music and woodworking lessons, overseeing sports and outdoor activities, organizing parties and picnics. "She never used the strap," a former student remembered.

The Gjerdin children, Gunnar, Martin and Harriet, attended Doriston school. The family arrived in the inlet in 1924 from Sweden via the US. Oskar Gjerdin, with the help of his wife Albertina, carved a "stump ranch" from the wilds, built and repaired boats, grew a huge garden, raised sheep and, according to the *Peninsula Times*, "cured his own tobacco for over forty years."

Gunnar and Martin spent their lives at Doriston. They built their own fishing boats, the *Echo* and the *Orivo*. They dredged out a boat harbour in front of their property and constructed a breakwater to protect it. In winter, they logged. For electricity, they put in a Pelton water wheel. Their gardens were legendary and so was their hospitality. Everyone on the inlet knew the Gjerdins.

Gunnar, in particular, as the oldest inhabitant, became known as the "mayor" of Doriston. He was an open-hearted soul, quick to drop his tools and greet or entertain visitors. He loved parties, and the Gjerdin home was the site of an annual event, known as Doriston Days, as well as many other, more impromptu celebrations. Social functions were always marked by an abundance of fresh local foods.

Gunnar was ninety when he died, in December 2003, having outlived his younger brother and his wife, Cherry. In January, a final party was held in his memory at Egmont Community Hall. The place was packed. Friends sang songs in his honour, read poems, reminisced. Many tales were related of Gunnar's garden and his frequent gifts of giant vegetables. One speaker described how she'd teased Gunnar by bringing along an oversized zucchini. "This is one of my smaller cucumbers," she told him. A short while later Gunnar appeared, pushing a wheelbarrow filled with an enormous cabbage. "This is one of my smaller Brussels sprouts," he retorted.

The final eulogist at the memorial asked the audience to join her for the Doriston national anthem, composed by none other than Gunnar Gjerdin. The entire hall rose and, to the tune of "O Tannenbaum," belted out: "Oh, Doriston, oh, Doriston, ta-ta-da-da, oh, Doriston." It was Gunnar's last laugh.

Salmon Inlet, south of Narrows, is wide and rugged, and has seen much industrial activity over the years. Naturally enough, only the more determined tourists head there. A major BC Hydro transmission line runs along the inlet's northern slopes, on its way to Vancouver Island. A smaller line, at sea level on the south shore, conveys power from Clowhom Dam to the Sunshine Coast and beyond. Despite these blots on the landscape (and many clear-cut scars), there's still plenty of drop-dead scenery here: sheer granite

SALMON INLET'S CLOWHOM DAM PROVIDES POWER TO THE SUNSHINE COAST AND BEYOND.

cliffs, tumultuous waterfalls, receding snow-capped ranges. At Salmon's eastern end is Clowhom Lake, a twelve-kilometre extension of the inlet that just happens to hold fresh rather than salt water. Clowhom reaches to the flanks of 2,600-metre Mount Tantalus, highest peak in the region.

We consider kayaking into Salmon, but campsites are few and far between. There is one marine park, Thornhill Creek, perched under the hydro line about halfway down. Farther along, all the best camping spots are privately owned or occupied by the forest industry. One cool, clear Sunday in September we decide to borrow a small outboard-powered open boat and spend a day cruising the inlet instead.

On the way we see large flocks of up to fifty female common mergansers feeding together on small fish. Juvenile harbour seals are everywhere. We pass few human habitations, though: a decaying summer camp just east of Nine Mile Point, several fish farms on the northern shore. Ninety minutes later, without seeing a single other vessel, we close in on the head of the inlet.

To our left, a dramatic torrent leaps from a cleft in the rock. This is the mouth of Misery Creek, and the bay just beyond is Misery Bay. I'm not sure where all the misery came from, though the area has seen heavy logging operations over the years. In the 1920s, Regina Timber crews used locomotives to haul out the choicest trees but had difficulty getting the primitive "cars" down the last section of track, which was at a forty-five-degree angle. A huge "snubbing engine" with a three-metre drum was installed at the top of the incline and each loaded railway car attached to it by cable before being gingerly spooled to the water where the logs were dumped. The company went bankrupt and was taken over by Gustavson Brothers Logging, which maintained a sizable camp near Misery Creek until 1934. Eventually, two engines and seventeen cars ran over eleven kilometres of track.

On the opposite shore, outwash from Sechelt Creek has formed a sandy alluvial fan that almost cuts the inlet in half. A dock leads to a small logging camp, and you can walk up a road beside the creek to a trail that leads past a series of artificial salmon-spawning channels.

At the very head of Salmon Inlet, the industrial presence intensifies. Interfor has a large camp, and a vast network of logging roads runs back into the valleys to the east. And then there's the hydroelectric dam. I guess we're lucky we don't have a pulp mill, too, as Clowhom Lake—one of many spots in BC where a large, elevated body of water empties into the ocean via some type of cascade—is perfect for generating electricity. G. Frank Beer of the Industrial Power Co. of BC wanted

KATHERINE AND COASTWISE JOHN DAFOE IN SECHELT INLET

very much to build a pulp mill at Clowhom in the years before World War I, but the Powell River mill went into operation first and there was no demand for a second facility in the area.

Clowhom Falls must have been a spectacular sight before the first dam was built, in 1950. It was quite a tourist attraction. In 1931, US lumber king Frederick Leadbetter, who owned the pulp mill at Port Mellon, purchased a shingle mill beside the falls and turned it into Clowhom Lake Lodge, which still exists. There were several fishing lodges at Clowhom, in fact, in the 1930s, '40s and '50s; the *Comox*, a Union Steamship boat, ran day trips from Porpoise Bay to the falls, then through the Skookumchuck Rapids to Pender Harbour and back to Sechelt on the Strait of Georgia side.

At the lodge's dock we tie up and go looking for someone to ask how we can get to the lake. Nobody is around. We cross the steep, landscaped property, climbing past unusual old trees, attractive cottages and the main lodge, a two-storey, six-bedroom cedar affair built in 1980. Soon we're right next to the dam, beside a bridge over bare rocks where the mighty falls once tumbled. The original dam and powerhouse were upgraded in 1958 and, while small by BC Hydro standards, still supply thirty megawatts of power.

We follow the road up to the lake, where we can see a distant helicopter plucking logs off a hillside. Walking back to our boat to prepare for the ride home, we pass two houses for BC Hydro employees. Only one is occupied these days, by the dam's operator and his wife, who are relaxing in their sunny yard. They tell us that the powerhouse is undergoing a refit and the lake level is lower than usual. They get out by boat once a week to do their grocery shopping in Sechelt. They love the peace and quiet (when there's no nearby logging, that is), own chickens and picked 300 peaches from their two large fruit trees this year. It seems like a good life for the right kind of people.

Over the past eight years Katherine and I have made many forays by kayak and boat into Sechelt Inlet. Each December, for instance, we venture through the Skookumchuck in a Boston whaler with our friend John Dafoe, a local guide who goes by the nickname of Coastwise John. Our task is to enumerate seabirds for the annual Christmas bird count organized by the Audubon Society.

All the camping areas on the three inlets are impressive. Most have attractive, rustic tent sites, pebble beaches, streams (water must still be boiled or treated), pit toilets and fine views. Six are part of Sechelt Inlets Marine Provincial Park:

Piper Point, Skaiakos Point, Halfway Beach and Kunechin Point on Sechelt Inlet; Thornhill Creek on Salmon Inlet; and Tzoonic Narrows on Narrows Inlet. Another three—Nine Mile Point, Oyster Beach and Tuwanek Point, all on the east side of Sechelt Inlet—are now part of recently established Mount Richardson Provincial Park. The sites are located a couple of hours' paddle from each other or less, and arranged so that visitors can make circuits or loops through the region without retracing routes or camping twice at the same place.

In summer, if we're paddling, we usually cross the wide mouth of Salmon Inlet, where waters can get rough, early in the morning, then stop and enjoy the coves and outcrops of Kunechin Point. We always see seals and other wild creatures. On one occasion we drifted close past a group of four sea lions. Everywhere in the inlet we keep our eyes peeled for pictographs—red ochre images left on the rocks ages ago by the Sechelt people.

Back in Sechelt, over a drink, perhaps, on the waterfront patio at the Lighthouse Pub, we marvel at how lucky we are to have this outdoor playground at our fingertips. These protected ocean fjords, we agree, with their beauty and wealth of history, are one of southwest BC's best and most unsung marine destinations.

SHELTER FROM THE RAIN AT KYNUMPT HARBOUR

Paddling with Wolves

Queens Sound on the central coast

Elaine points down the shoreline. "Look," she says, in some surprise. "A dog."

How can there be a dog here, I think, on this forested speck of rock at the extreme edge of BC's central coast? Where the heck are its owners? We haven't seen another human soul for days.

Then the rest of us spot a large, rather wet canine form sauntering away. Our islet is only about a hundred metres long, so we soon catch sight of the animal again, coming toward us from the opposite direction. The creature is dark brown and black in hue, and it slinks down the beach past our camp, tail between its legs, fearful but still willing to come within ten metres of a group of four humans. A short distance away it stops and scrutinizes us with a long, steady stare before disappearing behind some rocks.

We break out in exclamations. A wolf, a young wolf! And so close! Later we spot it swimming across to a neighbouring island, swivelling big ears in our direction from time to time. The animal strolls along the far shore with seeming nonchalance before merging into the trees. Should we be concerned? We recall the July 2000 incident on Vargas Island in Clayoquot Sound where a young kayaker, asleep, was attacked by a wolf and required dozens of stitches to close the wounds to his scalp.

We are kayakers ourselves; on this trip Katherine and I, in our single boats, are travelling with our friends Elaine and Mike from Roberts Creek, who have a double. Although we know lots of people on the Sunshine Coast who like to kayak, only Mike and Elaine start grinning like maniacs and vigorously nodding their heads when we describe the multi-day forays into the coastal wilderness that we've made or are planning for the future. They're experienced outdoor types who do a lot of backcountry camping and overseas trekking—as well as plenty of paddling, of course.

We've taken BC Ferries' Discovery Coast route from Port Hardy to Bella Bella, unloading our boats and mountains of gear at McLoughlin Bay and repacking it all on the adjacent beach. Then we paddle north up Lama Passage, past the old light station at Dryad Point, out into Seaforth Channel and around the north end of Campbell Island to Kynumpt Harbour, where we camp for the night. Our goal is to spend nine days exploring the remote splendours of Queens Sound and the Hakai Recreation Area. But things don't go exactly to plan.

The trip starts off well enough. We're elated to be on the water again, back in nature, living outdoors. A journey like this is hard work, with regular chores and frequent discomforts, but it also offers deep openings to savour the stillness, the birdsong, the changing moods of the water, the endless pulse of the tide—and to share these moments with friends. We eat well this first night: steak, fresh beans, pan-fried potatoes, beer, chocolate brownies for dessert. There's an old, derelict homestead behind our camp, where honeysuckle has run amok and thousands of bees buzz round the fragrant blossoms. In an overgrown orchard, cherry and apple trees are quilted with leathery lungworts. We cross fields of flowering cow parsnip and follow a short trail that connects Kynumpt Harbour to the broader vistas of Norman Morrison Bay.

It rains heavily in the night, dampening our spirits and our gear. Next morning we cross Raymond Passage in fog and, paying careful attention to the currents, cruise through rocky Rait Narrows at low slack and along Joassa Channel to Cree Point on the southern tip of Dufferin Island. Campsites are few and far between on this part of the coast, but we find a couple of square metres of level ground that have been improved over the years with firepits and driftwood benches. A kayaking couple from Seattle have spread themselves over three potential tentsites, but we shame them into moving some of their stuff and settle right in.

Cree Point is magical: a protected, shallow cove on the edge of Thompson Bay, where false azalea and copperbush bloom and huge cedar, hemlock and spruce trees are draped with old man's beard. Over the next two days we investigate Waskesiu Passage and Princess Alice Island to the west, and paddle out to the bays and beaches of southwest Athlone Island, on the edge of Milbanke Sound. Here we're exposed to open Pacific swells, which suck at the rocks with alarming voices, slurping and drooling like hungry beasts. The sun emerges from the fog, and the day even warms up enough for a cool, refreshing swim.

Omens are in the air, however. Equipment failures plague us, some the result of my own carelessness and lack of planning. A pair of glasses gets crushed. A canister of precious stove fuel mysteriously evaporates. Still, the weather holds and in a morning fog we pack up and leave Cree Point and work our way south to an archipelago of tiny islands at the eastern entrance to Thompson Bay. It's here that we see the wolf.

Although the Heiltsuk people, whose traditional territory this is, have been familiar with the coastal grey or timber wolf, *Canis lupus nubilis*, for millenia, remarkably little about its unique behaviour was known to science until recently. This wolf has adapted to its marine environment in extraordinary ways, swimming from island to island in search of black-tailed deer, fishing for salmon, and eating shellfish and the occasional marine mammal carcass. According to Chris Darimont, biologist and lead investigator for the Rainforest Wolf Project, and carnivore expert Dr. Paul Paquet, the project's senior scientific advisor, the BC central coast is one of the planet's best remaining wolf habitats. Its lupine denizens, which are slightly smaller than their inland relatives and often have a reddish colouring, may even differ genetically from other wolves.

The wolf project is funded mainly by the Raincoast Conservation Society, based in Victoria and Bella Bella. Darimont and his team travel widely in the region, sampling the DNA of coastal wolves by collecting their droppings, or scat. The goal of this research is to enumerate animals in a 2,500-square-kilometre study area and determine their movements and diet. Already it's becoming clear to Darimont and Paquet that BC's coastal wolves need large swaths of low-elevation old-growth forest to survive and are threatened by extensive clear-cuts inflicted on the region by the logging industry.

We, meanwhile, decide to continue south while the weather remains calm. As soon as we quit camp the rain begins; after two hours we find ourselves also facing into a steady, unfriendly headwind. We paddle across open waters south of Stryker Island and negotiate a scary little tidal rapid hidden in the centre of Codfish Passage, one of the main channels entering Queens Sound. At the edge of Tiderip Pass (ominous name, that), unable to find any suitable places to stop and set up our tents, we pause, decide to cut our losses and beat a lengthy retreat to the previous night's campsite, arriving back cold, tired and exhaustively soaked.

Our marine radio issues stern warnings of gale-force southeasterlies and a rapidly dropping barometer. We're at a good spot, though, shielded from the open sea by a cluster of rocks and islets. To the north, a relatively calm lagoon and narrow, protected Louise Channel offer a safe exit should we need it. A saddle of sand and shell fragments, briefly submerged at high tide, connects our refuge to a larger island. We burrow into thick salal and scrub crabapple, which muffle the wind, and find a flat opening sheltered by a large hemlock, just big enough to erect two tents. A tarp slung over low, sweeping branches creates a kitchen. We're perched at the edge of the world, with ocean swells crashing over nearby reefs and surging through narrow openings between the rocks. We get a fire going and dry out a little and then the rain starts again. It doesn't stop for the next four days.

The conditions test us; staying warm, dry and cheerful is a challenge. Can this really be late July? We trade reading material and snacks, emerging now and then to cook meals and check the weather. One afternoon we paddle up Louise Channel to where a stream is marked on the chart. The crystalline water trickles out of a cleft in the rocks and flows through a miniature valley of green. After thirty minutes of pumping I look up and notice an alert, intelligent face watching us through a screen of branches with what seems to be a bemused expression. It's another wolf, a large adult by the look of it, and no more than six metres away. Though coastal wolves are sometimes described as tawny or rusty in hue, this one is also dark brown and black, with beautiful silver-grey highlights. As soon as we make eye contact, it turns and walks away without a backward glance, vanishing into the woods like a metallic ghost.

We're relieved to see that here, at least, the wolves, though curious, continue to show a healthy caution and respect. As we strive to remind each other, these carnivores are really no threat. Only two wolf attacks on humans have ever been reported in BC, and neither was fatal. In both cases, the animals involved had become habituated to human food and refuse, as had wolves implicated in attacks elsewhere in North America. Nevertheless, looking directly into the eyes of a creature capable of tearing you to pieces is an unnerving experience. These coastal wolves, Chris Darimont discovered, kill black bears for food; in fact, the larger animals form a startling 8 percent of their diet. The fact that wolves eat at the top of the food chain makes them what Darimont calls a "keystone" species. By protecting wolves we ensure that the entire ecosystem remains healthy.

Finally it's time to make the two-day journey back to Bella Bella to catch the ferry home. In a near-constant deluge, we paddle up Louise Channel, down Boddy Narrows and around Kingsley Point into Raymond Passage. Fortunately, the water is fairly calm until we turn into Kynumpt Harbour, where a vicious east wind hits us and almost drives us backward. It's a real effort to reach shore. When we get there, we have to quickly put up the tents in torrents of rain, on soggy ground, and change into dryish clothes to avoid hypothermia. As a final insult, the fly on Mike and Elaine's tent splits in two. Thank goodness it's only a two-hour paddle tomorrow to Shearwater, where there are hot showers and a nice restaurant.

On the last night, as I lie sleepless in my damp shelter worrying about all the things that need to happen before we get safely back home, the image of the wolf keeps coming to my mind. Its adaptation to this chill landscape is inspired. With our flimsy tents and tarps, fragile watercraft and few inadequate belongings, we aren't well adapted. On this coastline, the image suggests, everyday routines are illusions. The devices of modern life are out of reach. They can't help us here. We're offline, right off the grid. Reality begins in the rain and the wind with the sound of the surging waves—the world of the wolf.

A RARE WATERSPOUT IN MALASPINA STRAIT. *Garry Ehman photo*

Gusty Weather

Encounters with BC's distinctive winds

One September many years ago, when I was a novice kayaker, I went for a paddle in Indian Arm with two friends. This fjord burrows deep into the Coast Mountains from Burrard Inlet and forms a fine backdoor playground for Vancouver's outdoor types. It was a beautiful sunny morning with a fresh westerly—lots of small chop but nothing we couldn't handle. After crossing the arm and having lunch at Twin Islands Provincial Marine Park, we headed back toward our Deep Cove launch site. Dark clouds were gathering to the north of us, at the head of the fjord, but the sun was still shining and we expected no trouble on the return journey.

How fast the weather can change on the BC coast. Partway across the arm, the westerly suddenly died and an eerie lull engulfed us. All the pleasure boats in the area seemed to be racing back to port. Did they know something we didn't? I felt a different breeze, a colder one, at my back, coming from the northeast. Initially, we were driven over the water like leaves, and I was exhilarated. But this new wind was getting stronger by the minute, and the waves were rising. My excitement soon turned to alarm.

At first, I could track well with my rudder and soon found myself far ahead of my friends, who had smaller, rudderless craft. "Turn into the waves," one of them yelled at me. But I was afraid to. It meant putting the boat broadside to some big water. I thought I could outrun the weather. Then the wind really started to howl, blowing whitecaps horizontally off the waves. It began to rain. Visibility decreased. I don't know how strong that wind got—sixty kilometres per hour? eighty kilometres per hour?—but it was gusting so violently I thought I might be launched into the air. All my fears had come to pass: I was far from land, alone and terrified, in the midst of a violent storm.

Most kayaks are remarkably stable when pointed into the wind and waves, but they can fishtail badly if nature's forces are being hurled at them from behind. A sudden mighty blast of air swerved my vessel sideways, where it was slapped by a humungous wave. Next thing I was upside down beneath the boat. I got out okay, losing my paddle and expensive sunglasses in the process, and clung to the side of the kayak. I had a paddle float, used for self-rescues, but without the paddle itself (and with no spare aboard), my chances of getting back in the kayak were zilch. My mind was strangely calm. The worst had happened; now it was just a matter of time before I was rescued or hypothermia claimed me.

Thankful for my bright yellow life jacket, I pushed myself out of the water as far as possible and waved at distant passing boats. They continued to pass. After about twenty minutes, the last vessel on the horizon veered my way, and its skipper, watched by a couple of saucer-eyed passengers, threw me a line. I clambered aboard, kayak in tow, and we headed to the nearest dock, which happened to belong to a yacht club. With difficulty—and despite the protestations of a club member—I jumped ashore, then puked on the deck, narrowly missing the man's shoes. Half an hour later the storm passed. My buddies paddled in, laughing at their adventure. As we drove home, trees and powerlines were down. At Pitt Meadows, winds had been clocked at sixty-six knots (122 kilometres per hour). Two people died.

We have many different types of winds on the BC coast, but for the most part, the words we use to describe them are hardly inspired. The storm that did me in produced a few brief hurricane-strength gusts but was, in truth, a transient, local event. While recounting my experience in the months and years that followed, I often wished there was some dramatic term—typhoon, perhaps, or cyclone—I could use to bolster my description. But all I could really admit to was getting caught in a tempest and making a number of rookie mistakes, the worst of which was failing to have my paddle tethered to the deck rigging. Besides, we don't have typhoons or cyclones in BC.

In his 1984 book, *Heaven's Breath: A Natural History of the Wind*, Lyall Watson names almost 400 winds from all over the world. He mentions the apeliotes, a gentle Mediterranean southeasterly that the ancient Greeks portrayed as a young man bearing fruit. The black roller, according to his list, is a dust storm in the western US, while the hot bricklayer blows across southeast Australia. The names of the winds are lyrical—

poetic, even. The Gulf of Mexico spawns the chocolatero, a sandy squall. There is the dry chom of Algeria, the fierce churada of the Marianas Islands, the gentle Slavic dogoda and the gail-force Swedish frisk. Hurleblast, kogarashi, naf hat, reffoli, tarai, whirly—the world's winds blow on and on.

Nowhere in Watson's list, though, do we find any BC winds. This is a shame, as we have several with distinctive names. The Jervis express roars south down the inlet it's named after. A strong but short-lived southeasterly encountered at the mouth of Howe Sound is known as a duster. A fog wind is a fisher's name for a storm-force surge that sometimes smacks the northwest coast of Vancouver Island. And local First Nations languages, of course, have dozens of terms for specific winds; Northern Straits Salish, to name just one, has separate words for west, east, south, southwest, northwest, southeast and northeast winds.

Mariners name each wind for the direction it comes from. Prevailing summer winds in BC are usually westerlies, brisk but benign. In winter, icy outflow winds snarl down from the northeast, while stormy blasts circle around the Pacific to pummel us from the south and southeast. Meteorologists have wind words, as well. Anabatic winds, for instance, flow up the sides of the inlets by day, when the land warms more quickly than the water, while katabatic, or drainage, winds roll back down and out to sea at night. We have vicious gap winds, funnelled by landforms, and sneaky corner winds, which lurk in the lee of islands and headlands. But none of these are unique to BC.

Most people have heard of the dreaded Squamish—that gale-force scourer that wails down BC's narrow inlets in winter. As its name suggests, this wind was originally associated with Howe Sound, home to the Squamish First Nation and the town of Squamish. But the word is applied to any violent flow of cold polar air that gets channelled through the Coast Mountains to the Pacific.

Squamishes are most common in fjords oriented in an east-west or northeast-southwest direction. They can be wicked in Toba and Knight inlets, Portland Canal and Dean Channel. Bute Inlet, which reaches into the heart of icefields and high peaks, produces a notorious subzero outflow, often referred to simply as the Bute wind. When high-pressure ridges grip the BC interior and a big low lurks offshore, the Bute wind will exceed one hundred kilometres per hour (fifty-five knots) and be accompanied by deadly freezing spray. Gusts can be greater than 185 kilometres per hour (one hundred knots) and flatten forests. In Howe Sound, by comparison, where outflow winds often persist for three to five days in December and January, speeds usually reach fifty-five kilometres per hour (thirty knots), with gusts up to twice that mark. Squamishes lose their strength when out of the restrictive fjords and are rarely evident twenty-five kilometres offshore.

Another dangerous inlet wind is the williwaw, a local draft that suddenly drops from high ground, perhaps through a notch in the mountains, and swirls across the water's surface with enough power to flip a small boat. The origin of the word, used more commonly in Alaska, is unknown. Williwaws also occur in the fjords of Chile and in the Straits of Magellan.

A different type of BC wind, the Qualicum, can also be a danger to small craft. This is a fall or föhn wind: a warm, dry westerly like the chinooks that descend on the Prairies. (Some wet southwest winds that blow along the coasts of Washington and Oregon are also called chinooks.) Qualicums flow up Alberni Inlet and through an opening in the mountains of Vancouver Island. They lose their moisture over the high ground and then plunge with a seventy-five-kilometre-per-hour (forty-knot) vengeance on Qualicum Beach and the Strait of Georgia. A similar gap wind blows out of the Cowichan Valley.

(Simoom Sound, incidentally, on BC's central coast, is named after a wind, albeit indirectly. Those who have read Michael Ondaatje's *The English Patient,* and the lyrical account of African and Asian winds that the protagonist inscribes in his copy of Herodotus, will recall the legendary simoom, a searing North African desert wind. The name derives from the Arabic word for poison and was given to a British warship, HMS *Simoom,* which, in turn, was the source of the BC place name.)

The strangest wind formation I've ever seen in BC is a waterspout: a rapidly whirling, funnel-shaped column that descends from the base of a thunderstorm cloud and draws up water from the ocean. I've seen several, in fact, all in the Strait of Georgia. It was hard to judge the diameter of the spouts, as they were quite distant, but their height was several hundred metres: perfectly formed miniature tornados. They moved north at a rapid speed. Through binoculars I could make out turbulent white water where the spout met the sea. I was safe ashore at the time, but I wondered what it would be like to meet one in a kayak.

"Waterspouts are usually weak and fairly short-lived," says Roland Stull, of the University of British Columbia's atmospheric science program. "They don't really have a mind of their own. They just go where the ambient flow blows them. They could capsize a boat but they probably wouldn't tear it apart." Several are reported each year in the Strait of Georgia, Malaspina Strait or outer Howe Sound. Stull suspects that they are formed when strong gap or outflow winds encounter slower air in Georgia Strait and create swirling effects while at the same time being subject to updrafts from the convective clouds of a thunderstorm.

With their wild rotation speeds, which can exceed 185 kilometres per hour (one hundred knots), waterspouts may suck more than just water up into the air. And what goes up must come down. Rare Spanish frogs rained on England in 1987, courtesy of a waterspout; elsewhere in Europe, there have been reports of minnows, sticklebacks, sand eels, crabs, starfish, flounders and periwinkles descending on the peaceful countryside. Shrimp, squid and herring have fallen on India. "We could have it raining salmon," says Stull, "though they are pretty heavy." If a waterspout passes over land, much more dangerous objects can be drawn up to fall from the sky.

While advising the public to steer clear of waterspouts, Stull admits that, as a meteorologist, he'd be tempted to inspect one at close range. Personally, though, I've decided to give them a wide berth, if possible. I've already come close to flying with my kayak, in Indian Arm, and that's enough for me.

THE GOVERNMENT WHARF AT GAMBIER HARBOUR
WITH BOWEN ISLAND IN THE DISTANCE

West Howe Sound

Hidden treasures at the urban edge

Starting a kayaking trip in the shadow of a huge, steaming pulp and paper operation feels strange, and most paddlers never visit this part of Howe Sound. But it makes sense. There's a good launch site just south of Howe Sound Pulp and Paper's enormous Port Mellon mill, where local people keep small boats. We'll be sheltered from wind as we cross Thornbrough Channel and cruise along the east and north coasts of Gambier Island. And this area, so close to Vancouver, has plenty to offer visitors.

Port Mellon got its start back in 1909, when Pioneer Mills began producing coloured wrapping paper there, using power generated from nearby Rainy River. The plant has a disastrous history, closing repeatedly over the years as pulp markets collapsed. Owned today by Oji Paper of Japan and Canfor, Canada's largest forestry company, the mill is the most modern and pollution-free in BC. It still produces dangerous organochlorines, albeit in tiny quantities, while tonnes of ammonia, hydrochloric acid, hydrogen sulphide, acetaldehyde, methanol and sulphuric acid leave its smoke-stacks every year. And it's a notorious electricity hog, using more power each day than Prince Edward Island. The hill-sides behind the mill and for kilometres around have been heavily logged for decades.

Of more historic interest—to me, at least—is another Port Mellon institution, Seaside Park, a hotel built the same year as the mill by George Cates, whose False Creek shipyard also constructed the *Britannia*. Today, few have heard of this pioneer tourist attraction, which lured boatloads of holiday-makers until gutted by fire in 1933. It's hard to imagine the attraction of picnicking and bathing next to a pulp mill, but Seaside was a popular place. I have an old postcard dated 1911 that promotes the resort with an image of a genteel couple in a canoe, the lady with a parasol, the man wearing a tie. Girls in straw boaters and gay dresses tiptoe through the shallows in front of a large, elegant building encircled with ground and upper-level verandas. The hotel was rebuilt after the fire, then taken over by Canfor and eventually torn down in the 1980s.

We cross the channel opposite the mill, skirting dozens of log booms moored near Woolridge Island, and work our way along the east shore of Gambier Island. After about ninety minutes we reach Camp Latona, established by BC's Catholic churches in 1959 but sold to The Firs, a Washington-based evangelical group, four decades later when enrollments were declining and the camp too expensive for the churches to run. Just beyond Latona, at Ekins Point, are a pair of yacht club stations. There are fine views from there across Thornbrough Channel to the McNab Creek drainage and also up Ramillies Channel to the Defense Islands, where Howe Sound narrows to an inlet and the winds often become fierce. An old trail ascends from Ekins Point to Gambier Lake, one-third of the way up Mount Liddell, the island's highest peak at 930 metres.

Another half-hour paddle brings us to Douglas Bay on Gambier's northeast shore. There are places to camp, and a creek with a pretty waterfall, but a group of five other kayakers has already nabbed the best site so we continue on. Forty-five minutes farther south we pitch our tent at the head of Brigade Bay in a grove of ancient bigleaf maples. A well-used fire pit suggests that many travellers have lingered here over the years. Canada geese approach us on the beach, looking for handouts, and a gorgeous pileated woodpecker hacks away at a rotting stump close by our camp, completely ignoring our presence. Behind the maples we find traces of Charles Wiegand's old homestead. In the early 1900s he raised canaries, pheasants and Belgian hares at this pleasant spot, and kept deer in a pen. He grew violets and lilies-of-the-valley as a hobby, planted a garden and orchard, and dug an artificial lake.

Sadly, we are probably one of the last groups able to overnight at Brigade Bay. A 300-hectare parcel of land there, one of Howe Sound's last big chunks of privately owned coastline, changed hands recently and has been subdivided and partly logged. The site is now off-limits to campers. Thirty-four waterfront properties went on the market in 2004. On our visit, distant excavators are already putting in the first roads, bringing the landscape to that state of total annihilation that seems to be required before any modern land development project can proceed. In the future, I suppose, this section of coast will regain its natural beauty, though for now it has a truly damaged look.

In the evening we wander through the combat zone of shattered tree limbs and find a path that leads into a beautiful intact forest and over to Camp Artaban, the Anglican Church camp established in 1922 at the head of Long Bay (also known as Port Graves). Howe Sound, with its proximity to Vancouver and abundance of shoreline, has been popular with churches since 1907, when a YMCA facility, known today as Camp Elphinstone, was established near Langdale. Now there are dozens of camps in the region.

I hardly recognize Artaban, where I'd briefly worked as a teenaged "leader" over forty years before, but I remember the network of old trails that still exists in this area, to Lost Lake, Douglas Bay, Halkett Bay and Mount Artaban. And I remember the great trees, the thick underbrush and the moist, rich smell of the place. Perhaps these early experiences helped plant a seed in me that later in life grew into a love of the outdoors.

Across Ramillies Channel, the steep-sloped mass of Anvil Island rises in front of us like a giant's fortress. From the vantage point of our kayaks, the Howe Sound landmark seems well named. It's not difficult to imagine the fire god Vulcan shaping a piece of armour on the island's dramatic, horn-shaped peak. I've admired this monolith on numerous trips up and down the Sea-to-Sky Highway; this morning we're finally about to reach its forbidding shoreline.

We head to Daybreak Point, site of another summer camp, this one run by Marineview Chapel, an independent community church in Vancouver. Most of the island is too vertical for habitation, but a handful of cabins lines the pebble beaches at the south end. This was the only large island in Howe Sound that Captain Vancouver bothered to name when he

ANOTHER GAMBIER ISLAND GOVERNMENT WHARF, THIS ONE NEAR HALKETT BAY

passed through; he noted that, by keeping west of a line drawn from Anvil's Leading Peak through Passage Island at the entrance to Howe Sound, he could avoid the dangerous mud flats extending from the mouth of the Fraser River.

Despite its small size and relative isolation, Anvil was home to one of the sound's earliest and most interesting communities. The first pre-emption was filed on its southern tip in 1872. By 1887, Thomas Keeling and his sons had carved a flourishing farm out of the wilderness. Keeling discovered beds of fine clay on his property, which he sold to the Columbia Clay Company, and a substantial factory was soon stamping out bricks marked "Anvil Island" for Vancouver's booming construction industry. It burned down in 1912 but a second business, the Anvil Island Brick Company, kept producing until 1917. A few more settlers arrived after World War I.

Union steamships called with supplies and the mail. Anvil even had its own post office from 1896 to 1950.

East of Irby Point, site of the clay deposits, we drift along the southern shore, now lined by a handful of waterfront cabins. Keeling's property has been broken up and sold over the decades, though Bill Champside kept the big orchard and garden going until 1937, selling produce to workers at Howe Sound's mines and mills. On the east side of the island, round a low, mushroom-shaped promontory, a trail supposedly leads toward the ominous horn of Leading Peak, but we decide to leave this journey to another time.

Instead, we head south, feeling last night's final outflow winds brush coolly against our backs. Ahead loom the guano-encrusted bird sanctuaries of Christy Islet and Pam Rock. These are ecological reserves, and Katherine and I watch quietly from a distance as purposeful, low-flying cormorant platoons zip back and forth to unusual twig nests, built up like chimneys to heights of almost a metre. Shrieking gulls swirl overhead and pink-toed pigeon guillemots cling to cliff faces. About seventy harbour seals are resting on the reefs surrounding Pam Rock.

If we didn't know better, we'd never guess that a sprawling metropolis lies twenty-five kilometres southwest, just over the towering North Shore mountains to our left. We can see Vancouver's traffic, though, whizzing along the Sea-to-Sky Highway, on its way to Squamish and Whistler. We're glad we're sitting in two single kayaks in the middle of Howe Sound. It's not too difficult to imagine that we've paddled back to an earlier era.

Ahead of us, the bulky *Queen of Surrey* shudders out of Horseshoe Bay, a reminder that you still need a boat to reach the west side of the sound. From Langdale, the ferry's Sunshine

Coast destination, you can take a water taxi to Gambier and Keats, where a handful of residents live year-round. Public marine transport is a tradition in these parts. In the 1950s, before BC Ferries, there was the Black Ball Line, and before that, for almost sixty years, the red-and-black-funnelled vessels of the Union Steamship Company—especially the *Comox, Capilano, Lady Evelyn, Lady Pam* and *Lady Rose*—were a much-anticipated sight at the area's dozen small communities. Another passenger boat that graced west Howe Sound for years, and also functioned as a full-service travelling post office, was the *Britannia,* owned by Vancouver's famous Cates tugboating family and part of their Terminal Steam Navigation Company.

Today there are more boats on the sound than ever before. Indeed, the southerly sectors are abuzz with pleasure vessels in summer. On our trip, however, we have plenty of room to ourselves, both on water and on land; around Gambier, especially, we hardly see another soul. Many parts of northern Howe Sound manage to retain a rare feeling of remoteness, despite being near to the city.

On our southward journey we follow the same route that Thomas Keeling's son, Fred, would likely have taken when rowing back to his homestead after visiting his dad on Anvil Island; young Keeling eventually settled at Halkett Point, on Gambier's southeast corner. We round Halkett's sheer bluffs and spy our home for the night, Halkett Bay Provincial Marine Park, a pretty spot with simple campsites beside a sand and pebble beach. The sun finally comes out for the first time on our trip, and we decide to spend an extra day here, do some hiking and explore this unspoiled green heaven in more depth.

A network of trails leads south and west from the park to the summit of 614-metre Mount Artaban, to the United Church's

ENJOYING A QUIET MOMENT AT NEW BRIGHTON'S GAMBIER ISLAND GENERAL STORE

Camp Fircom and out toward Hope Point, the headland between Halkett Bay and Long Bay. Fircom is watched over by a giant cross that you pass as you climb the mountain; like Artaban, the camp dates from the early 1920s. Hope Point, studded with cottages today, has an even older history; a small settlement, complete with a school, formed here early in the twentieth century but did not survive the disruption of World War I.

The last day of our excursion is cloudless and hot, and we contemplate circumnavigating Gambier to get back to our put-in. Four headlands separated by three deep bays stretch southward like the paws of a great verdant Sphinx. Most of Gambier's residents cluster on the westernmost extremity, where the tiny communities of New Brighton and Gambier

Harbour are served by roads, a store, government docks and a regular water taxi. A high-pressure ridge is building, though; rather than risk a long trip across exposed waters into a strengthening westerly, we ride that wind instead, aided by a flooding tide, back the way we came, resting en route at Douglas Bay. After about four hours we're once again passing under Port Mellon's belching smokestacks, with fish and chips and glasses of beer only a short drive away.

Two months later, we return to west Howe Sound, though near the Strait of Georgia and farther south. We put in one evening beside the harbour at the little town of Gibsons and, with a backdrop of Soames Hill and Mount Elphinstone to enjoy, paddle up and across Shoal Channel to Plumper Cove Provincial Marine Park on Keats Island. The mainland shoreline, though picturesque, is built up now from Gibsons through Granthams and Hopkins landings all the way to Langdale; dozens of boaters are out after dinner, fishing and fooling around. Keats is tranquil, though, and next morning, in a lemony dawn, we emerge from our tent and prepare for a paddle around the island. The water is high, making it easier to launch, and we should be able to catch an ebb tide south. Perhaps, if conditions look good, we'll make it out to the Pasley islands in the mouth of the sound.

From the pebble beach below the campground, we look north to a horizon jammed with mountains, rank upon rank, from the modest heights of Gambier Island to the peaks of the Tantalus range and the snow-capped volcanoes of Garibaldi Provincial Park. It's a view that has become so familiar, after years of riding the ferry to Vancouver from my Sunshine Coast home, that I rarely pay it much attention. But today, from this unfamiliar perspective, the true beauty of Howe Sound hits home.

We begin this venture by skirting the northern coast of Keats, passing the summer cottages at Melody Point and the open fields of Corkum's farm, a familiar landmark for ferry passengers and one that has been transformed in recent years into yet another religious summer camp, this one for families. The entire island, in fact, is a Christian funfest in summer. BC's Baptist churches have owned the southwest portion of Keats since 1926 and operate a big camp there while leasing much shoreline property to individual cottagers. BC Ferries runs passenger-only service from Langdale to Keats Landing, where the Baptist camp is located, and to the resort community of Eastbourne, which faces Bowen Island.

Keats is a small place, really, only two kilometres wide and just five kilometres long; a circumnavigation only takes a few hours. By mid-morning we've reached the government dock at Eastbourne on Collingwood Channel. This rustic spot, wouldn't you know, got its start as a church camp in the 1930s; today about 150 private summer homes cluster above a series of pocket beaches. We rest on Maple Beach then stroll dirt roads, dodging residents in electric golf carts and passing the Old Lodge, once a general store, now a rental cottage and reportedly home to a ghost.

Just south of Eastbourne we must make a choice. Do we cross kilometre-wide Barfleur Passage to the Pasley Group, or not? In summer, strong inflow and outflow winds develop in Howe Sound, especially in the constricted northern section between Anvil Island and Squamish. Indeed, a small-craft warning is in effect today. It seems crazy even to be

ON THE WAY TO MT. ARTABAN, GAMBIER ISLAND

contemplating a crossing, but the waters ahead of us, protected from the southerly breeze by the bulk of Bowen Island, are fairly calm, and we decide to dash over. Fifteen minutes later we're in the lee of Ragged Island; another short paddle brings us to the western shore of Pasley Island.

The Pasley Group is about as isolated a marine environment as you can find in greater Vancouver. There are six main islands, all privately owned, and some beautiful summer homes have been built. The archipelago is a kind of mini–Gulf

Islands, replete with tiny coves and cliffs and beaches—a refuge for the city's wealthy. Many homeowners on the most exposed islands—Worlcombe and Popham, especially, which once served as bases for whale and seal hunters—rely on wind generators for their electricity.

Pasley itself, the largest island, two kilometres long and one kilometre wide, was long owned by Vancouver's dynastic Bell-Irving family. Henry Ogle Bell-Irving made a fortune in the BC salmon-canning industry, bought the island in 1909 and made it a summer campground for his clan. Upon his death, in 1931, Pasley went up for sale, but no buyer could be found. Finally, in 1950, Henry Pybus ("Budge") Bell-Irving, Henry Ogle's grandson and a former BC lieutenant-governor, formed a syndicate and purchased the property for $25,000. The island is now owned corporately by a group of shareholder families (in much the same way that Hernando Island near Lund is held).

Casual visitors are not exactly encouraged in the Pasleys, but on one islet, connected by a spit, or tombolo, to Hermit Island, we spy a sign I thought I'd never see: "Private Island. Picnickers Welcome." This one place, known locally as Arbutus Island, has been reserved for the travelling public, and we gratefully beach our kayaks, step ashore and eat lunch in the shade of an arbutus grove, observed by two curious young deer.

Afterward I paddle round Hermit, which has long been associated with another well-established local family: the Tuppers. It was named after an earlier occupant, though, whose driftwood cabin was surrounded by the grisly skulls of all the seals he'd dispatched for food and clothing. Reginald Tupper, a grandson of Sir Charles Tupper, the Canadian prime minister, bought Hermit in 1926 after he and his wife got to know the area while visiting the Bell-Irvings. His son, David, strata-titled the island in 1968. Several pretty cottages have been built over the years, some with fine stonework. As I pass by I can't help contrasting the pleasant life of Hermit's current residents with that of the hermit himself, who apparently drowned while rowing his homemade boat to Gibsons for groceries.

We wait for the tide to change, then, with the wind behind us, scoot back across Barfleur Passage, past Preston Island, to Keats. Soon we're slipping between Home Island and the southern tip of Keats to enter Shoal Channel. The steep bluff overlooking Gibsons harbour is to our left. We contemplate a detour to town for treats but decide to head back to Plumper Cove, then later that afternoon hike to the old Corkum farm, lured by a rumour that a small gift shop there serves cappuccinos. And so it does, but not on Fridays or Saturdays, when the campers aren't present. Today, naturally, is Friday. A friendly staffer at Barnabas Family Ministries sells us cold drinks and lets us wander around and take photos. Barnabas owns a part interest in the farm and caretakes the idyllic landscape, where sheep roam and orchards burst with apples.

It's worth spending an extra day on Keats just to go hiking. A fairly well-marked system of trails, all on private land but maintained as fire evacuation routes, extends across the entire island. Visitors are welcome to use it. One lovely path leads to Lookout Peak, which has extravagent views of Gibsons and the Pasleys. We also walk the gravel four-kilometre Keats-Eastbourne Road; even on a summer Saturday, not a single vehicle passes by. From the Keats camp headquarters near the wharf at Keats Landing, jovial staff direct us to the Salmon Rock trail to the western tip of the island.

As I stand on the rock and look out at the Pasleys, I realize that yesterday, for once, we chose the right time to make our crossing. Today Barfleur Passage is a blizzard of whitecaps. Though the haze of Vancouver, just thirty kilometres away, is clearly visible on the horizon, the little island group seems as distant and unreachable as the west coast of the Queen Charlottes in a winter storm. It's a good reminder that, for all its civilized amenities, Howe Sound can revert to true wilderness in the wink of an eye.

FREIL FALLS ARE ONE OF THE HIGHLIGHTS OF VISITING HOTHAM SOUND.

Up Jervis Inlet

Paddling Hotham Sound and Princess Louisa

Dear Tara, Zoe and Angela:

We found your message!

We were taking a rest break in a tiny cove when out kayaking last month. I noticed a brown bottle lying on the beach complete with a cork and cap, which was strange, so I looked more closely. There was a note inside. Shouldn't you be stranded on a desert island or something? You'd sent that bottle off six weeks earlier from Doriston, in Sechelt Inlet. We were paddling in Hotham Sound, an offshoot of Jervis Inlet, only twenty kilometres farther north. We're not the handsome young guys in Japan you were probably hoping to hear from, but we couldn't resist responding to a genuine message-in-a-bottle. Hey, your note made it through the Skookumchuck Rapids, at least.

THE VIEW DOWN JERVIS INLET FROM MALIBU CLUB AT THE ENTRANCE TO PRINCESS LOUISA INLET

We began our trip at Egmont, after a sleepless night at the nearby Klein Lake campsite, where yahoos partied all night long. It was a beautiful morning, calm, with a favourable tide, and we paddled across Jervis Inlet and north to Harmony Islands Provincial Marine Park, about a three-hour trip. Do you know Jervis? The waters there are very deep—over 660 metres in some locations, more than four times the height of Vancouver's Wall Centre. Thinking of this as you scoot across the surface is spooky; if you dropped your glasses here, they'd still be falling twenty minutes later. It's no wonder that submersibles and other underwater gadgets are tested in these dark, icy abysses.

North of Hotham Sound and Egmont the inlet narrows and its sides steepen as it zigzags more than sixty kilometres into the tight embrace of the Coast Mountains. There are some neat places along the way: Vancouver Bay, overhung by the rock faces of Marlborough Heights, where mountain goats roam; the bird-rich estuary of the Brittain River; Deserted Bay, where the Sechelt First Nation once had a large village, Tsonai, and still maintain a centre where young people can learn about traditional culture. Then, near the head of Jervis, there's the easy-to-miss entrance to another, smaller inlet, one famous far and wide for its beauty. This, of course, is Princess Louisa, celebrated for the lacy cascades that tumble down its sheer granite cliffs and for its enclosed, otherworldly serenity.

Back in Hotham Sound, we found the Harmony Islands very attractive also, but not too useful to kayakers, as landings are difficult and campsites virtually non-existent. After much searching, we located two square metres of semi-flat ground barely above high water where, with a bit of rock picking, we could pitch a tent. Despite its deficiencies, we grew fond of this spot. Extravagant black lilies grew all around, and a pair of rufous hummingbirds sipped on the pink urn-shaped flowers of the false azalea, which flourished in the woods behind us.

In the distance, we could hear the roar of the main attraction: Freil Falls. Harmony Islands Park seems to serve primarily as an anchorage for boaters who come to see this spectacle. And the falls are astounding. They boil over the lip of Freil Lake, perched 500 metres above Hotham Sound in a hollow beneath 1,465-metre Mount Calder. The main stream divides into two; one branch makes a vertical plunge of about 200 metres. The tributaries recombine, pass through a boulder garden, then make another big drop before bounding over the beach to the ocean.

You can glimpse the upper falls from the ferry that crosses Jervis Inlet from Earls Cove to Saltery Bay. But from a small boat, close up, you get a real eyeful. In most countries, this torrent would be a national heritage site; commercial sightseeing vessels would be jostling each other for the best view. Here in BC, thank goodness, it's just another waterfall.

After an uncomfortable night at our blanket-sized campsite, we set off to explore Hotham's upper reaches, which are bounded by cliffs in many places, but also by rocky beaches and a broad estuary of grass. Lots of oysters here, if you like them, though the shells can be tough on kayak hulls.

That evening we vowed to look for a better campsite and found a great one on the east side of the sound, just north of the park, where a stream trickles into one end of a small beach. The following day we paddled across Hotham, rounded Elephant Point and meandered along the shores of St. Vincent Bay, with its summer cottages and oyster leases. An innovative acquaintance of ours, Gus Angus, runs Totem Seafoods here, farming Pacific salmon instead of Atlantic, the usual species, and raising unusual creatures such as wolf eels and sablefish (also known as Alaska black cod) on an experimental basis. Naturally, we dropped by to say hello.

Next day it was time to leave. Most people will tell you that local waters are usually calm from dawn to about eleven a.m., and that's when kayakers should do their travelling. And it's true—usually. This sunny morning, however, had produced a stiff westerly by 8:30 a.m., just as we were approaching the steep, exposed bluffs of Foley Head. Soon we were facing a confusion of metre-high waves and were forced into a tiny cove to wait the weather out.

We stayed there all day, with knots in our stomachs. If we got pinned down for more than twenty-four hours, our food

THIS PLAQUE NEAR CHATTERBOX FALLS IN PRINCESS LOUISA INLET PAYS TRIBUTE TO PARK BENEFACTOR "MAC" MACDONALD.

would run out. In the cove we found your note, which cheered us up. We were beginning to feel that we should dispatch a bottle ourselves—and that our message should read "HELP!" But the wind died down a bit around six p.m., and we beat our way through scary waves round the headland and began the two-kilometre crossing of Jervis. As we got into the wind shadow of Nelson and Captain islands, the waves subsided, and by the time we reached Egmont, the waters were almost calm.

We looked up Jervis Inlet as we passed and thought what a daring trip it would be to paddle to the head. But there are easier ways to get there. Bryce Christie of Sunshine Coast Tours makes regular day trips to Princess Louisa on his twelve-metre boat *Topline*. It's also relaxing to head up on the 325-passenger *Malibu Princess*, owned by Young Life, a US-based fundamentalist Christian organization that runs Malibu Club, a resort located at the inlet's entrance. With its swimming pool, thirteen-hole frisbee golf course, gymnasium, performance centre, treetop ropes course, store, coffee shop and aquatic toys, Malibu offers young visitors, many of them from urban ghettos, a seductive blend of religious indoctrination and fun in the sun.

But you don't necessarily have to be a would-be Christian to go there. In May and September, Artesia Tours takes over the rustic log buildings to put on the Malibu Arts Retreat. Last year we attended this three-day event, where some of the region's best teachers offer courses in painting, drawing, photography, video, fabric arts, voice, dance, cooking, writing and song-crafting. I took my kayak, as well, and spent one whole day paddling around Princess Louisa, viewing wild things and visiting the powerful torrent of Chatterbox Falls at the end of the inlet.

Princess Louisa is a kind of paradise, despite the large number of visitors it gets these days. It was May when we were there, and the shoreline was dotted with blossoms: bleeding hearts, yellow violets, brilliant white bursts of Pacific dogwood. I spent twenty minutes watching a large black bear feast on the luscious foliage. Hundreds of swallows swooped and dove, while glaucous-winged gulls postured and screeched as part of their spring mating rituals.

And the arts retreat was great fun, for all ages. The food was excellent. There were all kinds of free performances. Malibu

MAIN STREET AT MALIBU CLUB ON PRINCESS LOUISA INLET

itself is a magical place. Built as a wilderness resort in the mid-1940s by US aviation tycoon Tom Hamilton, it originally catered to the Hollywood crowd. Young Life took over in 1953 and spent a lot of money there over the next half-century. The various sections of the resort nestle easily into the landscape of firs and lichen-covered rocks and are connected by a labyrinth of railed boardwalks. Corny but delightful totem poles decorate the wooden decks. The steep walls of Princess Louisa soar on either side.

Anyway, back to Hotham Sound. When we finally returned to Egmont after the dramatic paddle past Foley Head, we were more than ready for a cool drink at the Backeddy Pub. We met a fellow there who had been living out of a four-metre-long wooden dinghy for forty-five days. He'd rowed and sailed his way from Victoria and spent the last few days exploring the lower reaches of Jervis Inlet.

Isn't the BC coast amazing? Have a great summer.

Sincerely, Andrew and Katherine

The word "community" often has *broader meaning than just village or town. One of the chapters in this section, for instance, deals with the community life of a cannery, both today, as a "museum village," and formerly, as a more complex living entity. Islands—even quite large ones with many districts—can be communities, and two chapters here delve into island community life. And no book on the BC coast would be complete without visiting a First Nations community, in this case Lax Kw'alaams on the north coast, formerly Port Simpson.*

I've long been intrigued by places where the notion of community is not necessarily taken for granted, as it often is in cities. My first book, Promise of Paradise, *even looked at utopian communities in BC. While there are no utopias in this section, we're drawn, again and again, to settings where a lengthy human struggle is played out between the desire for peaceful self-sufficiency and the need to co-operate with one's neighbours to achieve common goals. This is, I recognize, an internal drama, but one I seem to share with many others.*

Coastal Communities

PART OF SAVARY ISLAND'S SOUTH BEACH SEEN FROM MACE POINT

Sunny Savary

Anarchy rules on BC's most unusual island

On paper, Savary Island's vital statistics sound brutal. This narrow, overgrown sandbar is only 450 hectares in size yet divided into 1,710 legal parcels of land. Over 400 of these lots have buildings on them. Savary is not served by BC Hydro or BC Ferries. There are no parks and few community facilities. Roads are rough, building regulations non-existent, and everyone relies on wells and septic fields. Why, you might ask, would anybody be attracted to such a congested, anarchistic place?

Okay. I've tried to scare you off. Several homeowners have warned me not to wax too enthusiastic about their hide-away. So, yes, eight-kilometre-long Savary is ridiculously over-subdivided. With fragile dunes, eroding cliffs and hoards of summer visitors, it could be an eco-disaster in the making. But Savary is also ringed by some of the province's best beaches. Its aquamarine waters are warm and clear. And its rustic, peaceful atmosphere, only 140 kilometres northwest of Vancouver, is very hard to resist.

Katherine and I reach this unusual island community the normal way—by scheduled water taxi from the small Malaspina Peninsula community of Lund. On Friday evenings in summer, however, Savary also boasts a "daddy" plane from Vancouver. This Friday, the chartered Twin Otter lands about 6:30 p.m., coasts to shore, makes a graceful spin and backs up to the beach. A sizable, dog-loving crowd has formed there to welcome fourteen shorts-clad daddies as they emerge barefoot and form a human chain to unload the baggage. One of them is Bruce Macdonald, Katherine's cousin, our host for the next few days.

Soon everyone disperses to their recreational abodes. Bruce and his wife, Dulcie, who arrived earlier in the week, own a comfortable cottage facing the main beach just west of the government wharf. They spend their annual vacations and most summer weekends on Savary, often joined by their children and a range of family friends. This time around, we're the fortunate ones.

Bruce and Dulcie are part of a proud island tradition. Although their cottage is the second on the site and not particularly old, their property—also referred to as the Herchmer or Rickards property—was one of the first to be occupied on Savary. It consists of two lots, originally acquired by Dulcie's grandparents, the Herchmers, who built a first cottage there in 1913 (the Rickards were Dulcie's parents). Her grandfather, the fiery Colonel Lawrence Herchmer, was the fifth commissioner of the North-West Mounted Police, from 1886 to 1900. He retired to Vancouver before his death in 1915, and his ceremonial sword hangs in the cottage hallway.

THE FRIDAY AFTERNOON "DADDY" PLANE FROM VANCOUVER ARRIVES AT SAVARY.

The fact that the Macdonald property is so close to the wharf—and on the most desirable part of the island, known as "the front"—is a sure sign of early ownership. Indeed, Bruce and Dulcie belong to an island aristocracy descended from the earliest landowners. They know everyone, and newcomers to Savary refer to them—and their cottage location—with a kind of respect bordering on awe.

While Bruce recuperates from work and Dulcie gardens, Katherine and I investigate the island by foot. We hike forest paths to Mace Point, the easternmost tip of Savary. Mixed flocks of sandpipers and plovers skitter ahead of us down the stunning white beaches. We visit the abandoned airstrip, have lunch at the Mad Hatter restaurant (now McElvis's Bar and

SAVARY ISLAND'S GOVERNMENT WHARF LOOKING WEST TO THE MALASPINA PENINSULA

Grill) and admire some of BC's largest arbutus trees. In the evenings we rejoin our hosts for delicious dinners or else accompany them to parties, for residents here maintain a busy social calendar in summer.

Savary's bizarre variety of homes is a marvel to us. There are tarpaper shacks and tidy ninety-year-old cottages built from island fir. Some structures, such as the Mint Teahouse, are freeform, built entirely from recycled and salvaged materials. A few landowners, freed by an absence of rules, have indulged their wildest fantasies, creating a fort with palisades and battlements, a fretwork-festooned Victorian-style home and a Gothic folly complete with turrets, leaded-glass windows and a ghost imported by invitation from Scotland (where its former residence had been torn down). Others have constructed the ultimate in dream homes, including a $3-million mansion with jade-green roof tiles. Our favourite, we decide, is the grand four-chimneyed log "cabin" built by early resident Bill Mace for A. E. McMaster, general manager of the Powell River pulp mill, in the 1930s. Forty years later, this U-shaped beauty was purchased by mining tycoon Norm Keevil, president of the Teck Corporation, and is still owned by the Keevil family.

The sheer number of island lots, which resulted from a pre-World War I get-rich-quick subdivision scheme that showed no regard for the island's natural topography or its limited water resources, worries many inhabitants. The tiny parcels, mostly fifteen by forty-five metres (about one-sixth of an acre) in size, were originally sold at the Pacific National Exhibition and through newspaper ads, often sight unseen, for ten dollars down and ten dollars a month. Wealthy Vancouver families often bought several adjacent properties, and the list of Savary's current landowners reads like a west coast *Who's Who.* Lots were passed along from generation to generation; today many are still unseen by their owners. What would happen to the fragile environment, islanders wonder, if a few hundred more of those 1,300 empty lots were to be developed?

The man most responsible for Savary's strange predicament is long dead, of course. George Ashworth, a crime reporter with the Vancouver *Daily Province,* visited the island with a photographer in 1910. Ashworth was enchanted by what he found, and his first impulse was to package that enchantment and sell it to as many people as possible. Together with his entrepreneurial brother-in-law, C. R. Townley, and Townley's real-estate partner, Harry Keefer, he bought part of the island from its owner, US lumber baron Harry Jenkins. The three-some surveyed their land into small lots and then embarked on an aggressive marketing campaign to attract Vancouverites to "the Catalina of the north." An early customer was another Ashworth brother-in-law: Colonel Herchmer.

Before Ashworth arrived, Savary had been virtually uninhabited. Known to the Sliammon people as Ayhus, the double-headed serpent (perhaps because of its shape), the island was a First Nation summer camp, especially cherished for its abundant clams. No one has been able to identify the source of the name Savary, bestowed by Captain George Vancouver. The first white resident, in 1886, was sixty-nine-year-old Jack Green, who raised livestock and established a successful trading post. It was his gruesome murder, and that of his business partner, Tom Taylor, in 1893—plus the lingering suspicion that Green had buried a fortune on Savary—that initially attracted Ashworth to the island. Hugh Lynn, an itinerant ne'er-do-well, was eventually hung for the notorious crime.

George Ashworth went on to find a different type of fortune on Savary. His real-estate crusade bore fruit—and settled the island's fate. By 1914, hundreds of lots had been sold and twenty-five cottages lined "the front." There was a school, and a store and post office run by Harry Keefer. A substantial dock was built that year, and a hotel, the eight-bedroom Savary Inn, opened and became the heart of the community's social life until it burned down in 1932.

Today about 800 people live on Savary in the summer; seventy of them, perhaps, spend the entire year there. Most properties are on the east side of the island, within walking distance of the government dock. The best beach fronts, of course—including Dough Row with its Shaughnessy-style summer places—are lined with homes. In the more sparsely

OPEN-AIR LUNCH AT THE MINT, A SAVARY TEAHOUSE CONSTRUCTED FROM SALVAGED WOOD

inhabited interior, narrow tracks snake through a dim forest of arbutus and second-growth Douglas-fir. Though many residents still get around on island taxis—flatbed trucks that roll all day from one end of Savary to the other—private vehicles are definitely on the increase.

We stay on foot and spend an afternoon exploring Savary's western end, an area that reminds me of the Caribbean with its splendid ocean views and winding, sandy roads and trails. We stop for an ice cream at Kassian's, a quaint, tiny store, and later end up at Indian Point, site of Ashworth's twenty-eight-room

Royal Savary Hotel, which opened in 1928 and was torn down in 1983. The Royal Savary era marked a high point in the island's recreational history. Avid young holidaymakers arrived from the city by Union Steamship, attracted by advertisements that compared Savary to a "South Seas paradise." In the 1930s and '40s, couples could come here for only twenty-five dollars a week, including meals, and enjoy tennis, swimming, badminton, beach golf, dancing and sheer relaxation.

In 1995, a dark cloud finally appeared over Savary, threatening the residents' summer idyll. The Trillium Corporation, based in Bellingham, Washington, owner of the only remaining large, intact piece of island property, applied to subdivide its land. This block, known as District Lot 1375, occupies the central third of Savary and harbours some extraordinary natural features, evidence of Savary's geological origins as a glacial moraine. The ancient sand dunes, which preserve wind-carved patterns that are thousands of years old, are of great scientific interest, as are the groves of red cedar and shore pine, the twisted Pacific yews and the rare plant communities of gumweed, red fescue and northern wormwood.

Despite the overwhelming opposition of islanders, the Powell River Regional District, which Savary is part of, enthusiastically endorsed the Trillium plan. After all, it would increase the district's tax revenues. The Savary Island Land Trust Society (SILT) was founded in 1997 to try to save the Trillium lands, described by biologist Kathy Dunster as the best example of a coastal dune ecosystem in Canada and home to many endangered plant and animal species. The same year, independent-minded islanders began the hard task of collaborating on an official community plan.

That plan hasn't seen light yet, but after five years of effort and endless lobbying, SILT's efforts did pay an enormous dividend. On April 3, 2002, the Nature Trust of BC, Environment Canada and the province announced the acquisition of a 50-percent interest in the Trillium lands and some other Savary properties. This $4.5-million deal, one of the great conservation coups in recent BC history, is designed to protect a total of 147 hectares of delicate duneland—one-third of the island—as an ecological reserve. A number of smaller private lots, including one four-hectare holding, have also been donated to SILT for conservation purposes.

The unheralded purchase does not guarantee Savary's future. The island was reaching "critical development thresholds" back in 1998, according to a Planistics Consulting study, and there are still those 1,300 or so empty lots. SILT is encouraging people to amalgamate them, and has a "lot consolidation" fund to help with the costs. It's still imperative that islanders and government agree soon on a comprehensive land-use plan. But local preservationists at least have a foundation to build on now. With any luck, Savary's residents will manage to save their island utopia and protect it for succeeding generations to enjoy.

THE NORTH PACIFIC CANNERY VILLAGE MUSEUM

North Pacific Cannery

Life at a restored fishing village

Each spring, when BC's canneries started up, a great mobilization took place on the coast. Families packed up and moved, bringing with them all the domestic goods they needed for a six-month sojourn. Often working at the same place year after year, they came by train and fishing boat and steamship. It was a migration as predictable, in its way, as that of the silvery torrent of salmon on which it was based.

The canneries, often located in remote areas, were complicated, self-contained worlds—complete communities. There were residential areas and various types of residences for the different workers. There were stores and offices and mess halls, often post offices and first-aid clinics. Water and electrical systems and, eventually, sewer lines were installed. Lengthy boardwalks linked all the different components together.

Over the years, 223 canneries have dotted BC's shores. At their peak, in the 1920s, about eighty plants were canning 2 million cases of salmon annually (more than 2,000 trailer truckloads). They were concentrated near the mouths of the great rivers—the Fraser, Skeena and Nass—and in Rivers Inlet, but could be found up and down the coast. Today, only half a dozen or so remain, mostly in Vancouver and Prince Rupert. An entire way of life has disappeared.

Faint echoes of that life linger at the Gulf of Georgia Cannery, a national historic site in Steveston, now a suburb of Vancouver. There are also echoes—stronger, perhaps—on Inverness Passage, 750 kilometres to the northwest, near the village of Port Edward just south of Prince Rupert. The North Pacific Cannery, also a national historic site, was built at this remote spot in 1889, only ten kilometres from the mouth of the mighty Skeena River. Miraculously preserved as a "cannery village museum," it has managed to retain a moody and compelling atmosphere along with a massive collection of artifacts and machinery.

As an added attraction, visitors to North Pacific can stay overnight in the heart of the cannery complex. One recent June, Katherine and I immersed ourselves in the village milieu by checking into the Waterfront Inn, a modest fifteen-room hotel located in what was once the bunkhouse. We were the only guests. We patronized The Salmon House, formerly the mess hall, an excellent little restaurant opposite the inn, and mingled with the museum staff, who live on-site, dress in blue workers' overalls and tie their hair up in no-nonsense, World War II-era red bandanas.

The voices of the past speak clearly here, especially at night, after the tour groups have left. "I lived for nine years at North Pacific, in the last house," recalls Teo Okabe in a museum guidebook. He built the communal bathtub—"one thing the Japanese can't get away without"—from cedar planks encased in steel and fired by an oil furnace. "We all got along very well," he remembers, "the Native people, the white people, the Japanese and Chinese when they got there." Okabe's house, now a dormitory for student groups, still stands, but not his bathtub.

North Pacific, like most BC canneries, was multi-ethnic and segregated. The Japanese and First Nations men were expert fishers; they owned or rented the majority of the cannery's sixty-seven fishing boats. Sail and oar were the main means of power until the 1930s, when gas engines became common. Native women cleaned the salmon and filled the cans. Most of the other cannery workers were Chinese, except the managers, technicians and office clerks, who were invariably white.

Communication between the different ethnic groups could sometimes be a problem, according to Terrace lawyer Terry Brown, who was born at North Pacific and worked there as a young man. In an oral-history excerpt from the guidebook, he relates how the Chinese foreman directed him to pile boxes of cans "chin" high. Later, he found himself in trouble. Finally, the foreman "put up ten fingers and we realized what he was telling us."

There were five canneries along this stretch of shoreline in the early years of the twentieth century. As you drive the winding road from Port Edward to the museum you pass a plaque marking the site of Inverness, the pioneer north coast operation, which opened in 1876, closed in 1950 and burnt to a crisp in 1973. Little remains, also, of Sunnyside, or of Dominion Cannery on Smith Island across the way. At the end of the road, Cassiar Cannery, or Caspaco (CASsiar PAcking CO), is mostly dismantled, the few habitable buildings occupied by squatters.

At North Pacific, however, quite a bit remains. Beyond the railroad tracks and salmonberry thickets are mouldering wharfs, docks and metal-roofed clapboard buildings, large and small, connected by boardwalks and cantilevered on wood pilings over the muddy shoreline of Inverness Passage. Maintenance and preservation seem like overwhelming chores.

Museum curator Sophie Cormier walks us through the main buildings. Because of the high cost of repairs and renovations, the development of the site must proceed in stages. Foundations, of course, are crucial, and Cormier shows me the old reduction plant, which is now the museum's large and well-equipped maintenance shop, beneath which scores of decaying pilings have been replaced and the floor surface rehabilitated. "Our next priority," she says, "is to create a proper dock," so that cruise ship passengers stopping at Prince Rupert can arrive at the museum in style. "Coming by boat," Cormier points out, "is the traditional way to arrive at the cannery and much more interesting than by bus."

The museum's directors and staff have had to be creative. When Skeena Cellulose, the Prince Rupert pulp mill, closed down in 2001, for instance, many young millwrights had their apprenticeship programs curtailed, thus jeopardizing their careers. The museum, however, which has a complete, original machine shop and is full of semi-functional equipment in need of constant attention, was able to get funding to continue the program. The tradesmen jumped in, rebuilt and repaired machinery, and fixed and improved all manner of other things. Everyone benefitted. Now, when the bandana-clad guides demonstrate how the canning lines work, conveyor belts whirl and cans pass along rollers and swivel down chutes. Cutting, filling, weighing, clinching and vacuum-sealing machines clank and turn. All that's missing is the smell of fish.

The complex was even larger in the old days. Over one hundred tiny cabins housing First Nations workers had fallen into ruin and were torn down. Two replicas, the latest additions to the museum, have recently been erected; staff are in the process of outfitting them with period artifacts. The main Chinese bunkhouse, a large two-storey affair, is long gone. But the cannery building itself, with its packing plant and fish shed, its huge posts and joists, dates from 1889, when it was erected by John Carthew, North Pacific's founder.

The cannery produced Walrus Brand salmon. In 1891, the year a landslide hit the plant, killing nine people, Carthew sold out to Henry Bell-Irving's Anglo-British Columbia Packing Company (ABC). Most of the remaining structures—including a salt warehouse and a can factory—were built in the early 1900s, during ABC's long tenure. The net loft was moved over from Port Essington in 1937 and now also serves as a theatre and performance space.

In the main cannery there's a wonderful photo exhibit on Port Essington, 20 kilometres distant on the south shore of the Skeena and once the region's metropolis. After 1906, when the new town of Prince Rupert sprang up to greet the arrival of the Grand Trunk Pacific Railway, Port Essington went into decline. Its paddlewheelers no longer churned their way up the Skeena to Hazelton. Its three canneries (with three more a short distance away at the mouth of the Ecstall River) were closed down by the 1930s. Its handsome buildings—hotels, churches and an ornate town hall with an observation tower—were abandoned or destroyed by fire. By the 1960s virtually nothing was left of the community.

THE CANNERY'S FISHING BOATS WERE RAISED TO THE MAIN WHARF IN WINTER AND STORED.

In 1968, ABC sold its North Pacific cannery, now obsolete, to the Canadian Fishing Company, which ran the reduction plant, making fish meal and oil. BC Packers bought the site in 1981, shut it down the following year and then gave it to the village of Port Edward in 1987. Since then, the members of the Northcoast Marine Museum and Port Edward historical societies have done an extraordinary restoration, winning a major award from Parks Canada.

Now 12,000 visitors a year wander past the canning lines and stumble over such unexpected delights as a huge array of colourful salmon-tin labels and an elaborate collection of fishing hoochies. Along the boardwalks, the office and store and workers' homes have been turned into walk-in exhibits. There's a gift shop, naturally. An excellent one-person theatrical performance, the "Skeena River Story," is repeated several times a day.

Finally, there's the watchman's house, an example of history in the making. Although only built in 1944, it has acquired significance of late as the childhood home of Iona Campagnolo, a well-known former politician and now BC's latest lieutenant-governor. "Cannery life was very interesting," Campagnolo recalled in a 1984 *Vancouver Sun* interview. "It was highly stratified between all the various groups that lived there because the nature of the times was very intolerant." As a teenager, the future Liberal party president and federal minister of state for fitness and amateur sport worked at North Pacific stacking lids into canning machines and, later, as a store clerk. "I look back on those days," she said, "as being exceptionally bright and beautiful."

THE ENTRANCE TO VON DONOP INLET IN FADING LIGHT ON A DAMP, DRIZZLY DAY

Cortes Culture

Maintaining a "high degree of self-expression"

By the time we arrive, the lineup for lunch is already forty-five minutes long. From the end of the snaking queue Katherine and I focus our attentions on a large canvas tent, beneath which we can spy a dozen tables groaning under a freight o' seafood. Islanders and tourists mill about in the sun, greeting, chatting, inspecting craft stalls and displays. Rolling grassy mounds (prehistoric First Nation fortifications, archaeologists suspect) support reclining families. From the back of a flat-bed truck the Cortes Singers belt out sea shanties. To the west, beyond a fine sand and pebble beach, tree-shorn Marina Island completes the scene.

The occasion is the Cortes Island Oyster Festival, held on the Victoria Day weekend in May at Smelt Bay Provincial Park, where we're camped. It's our third visit to the island, and we're here mainly for some kayaking, but this event, designed to promote a modest local industry, is definitely an added attraction. For fifteen bucks you can load up a paper plate with fresh grilled and glazed oysters, jalapeño clams, halibut ceviche, salmon pie, bread rolls and three different salads—plus, if you can juggle them, paper bowls of chowder (three types to choose from) and steamed mussels in a wine-flavoured broth. And then you can come back for raw oysters and, my favourite, steamed scallops—delicate little free-swimming shellfish live-trawled from local waters by a six-boat scallop fleet.

The oyster fest is pure Cortes, an uninhibited mingling of young and old, freaky and straight, together for an afternoon's feasting and fun. No alcohol is served (not in plain sight, that is), and nobody gets rude or out of control. There's frisbee golf, the course laid out on the tidal sand flats; a horseshoe tournament; a waitress relay race; and a thirty-dollar prize for the grower or finder of the day's biggest oyster. Later in the afternoon, as Gilbert Hanuse and Ron Pielle from the Klahoose First Nation village of Squirrel Cove belt out a raunchy "Kansas City," the food line shifts from shellfish to homemade ice cream. Two hours later, most everyone has left. By evening the tents are dismantled, garbage trucked away and the park grounds returned to respectability.

Respectability is good for a public park, but hardly a word one would associate with the community of Cortes. Unusual? Yup. Inimitable? Certainly. But respectable? Please! According to its own zoning bylaw and community plan, "Cortes is an island of spontaneity and natural organization," one whose residents desire a lifestyle that "allows for a high degree of self-expression." Located 210 kilometres northwest of Victoria at the north end of the Strait of Georgia, it reminds me of Saltspring in the 1960s. The two places make an interesting comparison. They are nearly the same size, roughly twenty-five

Above: MARY AND JIM BORROWMAN WITH ONE OF JIM'S WHALE SKELETONS AT TELEGRAPH COVE

Below: VICTORIA'S UPLANDS PARK HARBOURS ONE OF THE LAST REMAINING EXAMPLES OF A VALLEY-BOTTOM "PARKLAND" GARRY OAK ECOSYSTEM.

Above: HAIRY MANZANITA SHRUBS FLOURISH ON THE CURME ISLANDS IN DESOLATION SOUND.
Below: HARBOUR SEAL BONES IN A SECHELT INLET TIDEPOOL

FOREST GLADE NEAR MISERY BAY ON THE FAR REACHES OF SALMON INLET

Above: MALIBU CLUB AT THE ENTRANCE OF PRINCESS LOUISA INLET

Below: THE NET LOFT (RIGHT) AT THE NORTH PACIFIC CANNERY WAS TOWED OVER FROM PORT ESSINGTON IN 1

MAIN STREET: BOARDWALK AT NORTH PACIFIC CANNERY
NEAR PORT EDWARD ON A TYPICAL RAINY DAY

Above: THE BC FERRIES WATER TAXI HEADS PAST THE GRACE ISLANDS IN HOWE SOUND ON ITS WAY FROM LANGDALE TO KEATS ISLAND.

Below: JAMES BAY ON PREVOST ISLAND IN THE GULF ISLANDS NATIONAL PARK RESERVE

Above: THE *SPIRIT OF LAX KW'ALAAMS* IN SEA FOG AT THE HEAD OF TUCK INLET

Below: ON THE SHORELINE AT DINNER ROCK PARK LOOKING TOWARD MACE POINT ON SAVARY ISLAND

Above: AGATE BEACH IN NAIKOON PROVINCIAL PARK ON THE NORTH SHORE OF GRAHAM ISLAND

Below: THE "LOST SOULS' TREE" AT RAINBOWS GALLERY, QUEEN CHARLOTTE CITY, GRAHAM ISLAND

kilometres long and fifteen wide (although Cortes, at 125 square kilometres, is one-third smaller than Saltspring). Both have great rural charm. Over the years they've attracted similar types of settlers: farmers, originally, along with fishers and loggers, then artists and craftspeople, vacationers, retirees and modern-day back-to-the-landers.

But Saltspring, so close to Victoria and Vancouver, has swollen to a year-round population of over 10,000. The island has become a tourism centre and, in some areas, is developing a distinctly suburban character. Cortes, farther from the cities and harder to get to, has maintained a population of about 1,000 souls and hung onto its spirited rural ambience.

Some, mind you, would disagree. What with the logging and the tourists and newcomers from afar buying up land, they are convinced their island is going to the dogs. Many longtime inhabitants feel protective over their fragile paradise. Writer and naturalist Gilean Douglas—who came to Cortes in 1949 and died there in 1993, aged ninety-three—expressed her concerns about "progress" more than three decades ago, when electricity and a ferry service first arrived. "Our island was so unspoiled," she wrote in her 1971 Christmas letter, "so private and free, so dear and familiar to us all. Now I can go into a crowded store and not know a single customer's face ... Although I have lived here twenty-two years, sometimes I feel like a stranger now."

To casual visitors like us, Cortes remains one of the last bastions of climatic and cultural civility as one travels north on the BC mainland coast. Beyond here, where menacing tidal rapids lurk amid a dense cluster of islands, the landscape changes and logging starts in earnest. This is the northern limit for many plants, such as arbutus and juniper. Farther north the weather changes, too. Rains get heavier and cold winds whistle down deep coastal inlets.

The island (often spelled Cortez in earlier days) was named after Hernán Cortés, conqueror of Mexico, by the Spanish explorers Dionisío Alacalá-Galiano and Cayetano Valdés, who passed through this area in 1792 in the company of George Vancouver. Although their respective countries were at the brink of war, the three captains spent an enjoyable, co-operative three weeks together and had friendly exchanges with local First Nations groups. They named many of the region's features, including the sand-circled island west of Cortes, which the Coast Salish people knew as Chamadaska. The Spaniards called it Marina, after the conquistador's beautiful slave mistress, because it was nestled "under the shoulder" of its larger neighbour. (It was also known as Mary Island for over 50 years.)

Members of the Klahoose First Nation, part of the Salishan-speaking or Coast Salish fraternity, originally lived farther east, around the Redonda islands and Toba Inlet. They moved westward in the late nineteenth century and occupied most of Cortes as the threat of intertribal raiding receded; now Squirrel Cove, on the east side of the island, is their main village site. The southernmost part of Cortes was the territory of the Sliammon people, a neighbouring First Nation to which the Klahoose are closely allied.

Several small island communities grew up over the course of the twentieth century: Whaletown, base for two years for James Dawson, who with his ilk managed to kill most of Georgia Strait's humpbacks between 1866 and 1873; Squirrel Cove, the Klahoose community; Seaford, on the east coast, a former steamship landing; Cortes Bay in the southeast of the island; and Mansons Landing, the main population centre today, on the west side, where the first white settlers, Michael and Jane Manson, put down roots in 1886.

It's at Mansons Landing Community Hall, during the weekly farmer's market, that we see again many of the characters whose exuberance and outlandish attire we admired at the oyster festival. The hall, with a post office, library, playground and the Cortes Café, is a vibrant place on Mondays, Wednesdays and Fridays, when everything is open. On market day the place is filled with organic produce, dried fruits, preserves, teas, wonderful baked goods, ice cream, artful T-shirts, cards, moonshell rattles and other crafts—and a crush of eager buyers and vendors. At the entrance, island artist Dianne Bersea demonstrates the use of watercolour crayons and pencils, and displays some of her latest works: large colourful paintings of irises and California poppies. A representative from the Cortes Ecoforestry Society, which is working to establish a sustainable community forestry program on the island, hands out brochures and sells maps and memberships to passersby.

Next to the hall are the credit union and grocery store, and up the road, the elementary school and the Cortes Island Museum & Archives, with its tidy exhibits of pioneer and First Nations life. Down the road we find the excellent Tak Restaurant, Marnie's Books, a skateboard boutique and an open performance stage. Farther out, down leafy drives and pathways, an architecturally diverse array of homes and outbuildings (to say the least) lies hidden: driftwood castles, brightly painted Edwardian cottages, handcrafted cedar grottoes, lairs fashioned from recycled materials. Cortes, for instance, is the final resting place for numerous buses, some of which, lived in for thirty years or more, have sprouted appendages in the form of rooms and lean-tos and patios.

One bus we saw had a Volkswagen van body welded on top for a second storey, thus combining two '60s road icons in one sculptural unity.

It's not surprising that all this imagination and freedom should be concentrated at the south end of the island, beyond Mansons Landing, where the climate is benign and the coastline sprinkled with arbutus trees and century-old farms and orchards. Many visitors, in fact, head directly to this area to stay at the creative heart of Cortes, a retreat centre named Hollyhock, which has been influencing island evolution since it first came on the scene.

The nude frolickers in the hot tub have a view south to Hernando and Savary islands that's as good as it gets. In the vast blossoming garden, kitchen workers pick edible flowers to adorn the incomparable vegetarian fare. The voices of those taking the "Song as Prayer" workshop, led by performing artist Ann Mortifee and teacher Shivon Robinsong, trill and reverberate from the deep woods. This can only be Hollyhock, BC's original new-age resort, now famous across North America.

On one of our visits to Cortes, we spend an entire week at this island wellspring. Katherine has come to take Saskatchewan writer Sharon Butala's five-day class on the art of the personal essay. (Writers Bill Richardson and Sarah Ellis are also in attendance, leading a "reader's retreat.") I'm just tagging along. You don't have to enrol in a course to stay at Hollyhock; you can simply hang out and relax. Or you can use the twenty-hectare property as a base for investigating this isle of plenty. We have our kayaks along, of course, perfect for prospecting nearby shorelines.

Hollyhock started life as the Cold Mountain Institute, an Esalen-inspired sanctuary founded in 1970 by Richard Weaver, a student of Fritz Perls, where intensive Gestalt therapeutic techniques were taught and prominent figures—philosopher Alan Watts, poet Gary Snyder, author Margaret Atwood—came to give workshops and talks. Weaver died in 1975, but Cold Mountain continued until 1980 under the direction of well-known therapists Ben Wong and Jock McKeen, who eventually decamped to Gabriola Island and founded a resort and teaching institute there called The Haven.

In 1982, through the efforts of Greenpeace International co-founder Rex Weyler, Robinsong and a group of friends, Cold Mountain was reborn as Hollyhock. The centre kept the traditional personal-growth practises going, such as psychoanalysis, yoga and meditation, but added a wealth of other study areas: music, writing, cooking, gardening, massage, nature walks, kayaking—even midwifery and business management. Hollyhock's catchphrase is "a holiday that heals," and it has caught on. The resort's website listed 119 programs for 2004, everything from a midsummer circle dance to an investigation of "the soul of money," and included Ericksonian hypnotherapy, Iyengar yoga, applied shamanism, neurobiology, t'ai chi and basket weaving.

One morning, leaving the Hollyhock crowd to their inquiries, I paddle across Baker Passage to privately owned Hernando Island, a three-kilometre journey. A float plane is pulled up to a spit of gleaming white sand off Spilsbury Point. Luxurious boats linger offshore. In an ancient arbutus grove, a clutch of swank beach homes—cottage country's Millionaire Row—face directly into the high-peaked maw of Desolation Sound.

WHALETOWN'S TINY POST OFFICE IS OVER ONE HUNDRED YEARS OLD.

Hernando is flat and wooded and surrounded by beaches, like Savary Island. It was settled early, in the 1880s, and by 1892 had a population of forty homesteaders. The Campbell River Lumber Co. actually took the trouble to put in a railway logging operation there in the 1910s—hard to believe considering the island's five- by three-kilometre dimensions. Over the decades most settlers left, and in modern times Hernando narrowly escaped several attempts to turn it into a massive resort complex. It was eventually bought by a consortium of wealthy individuals and subdivided into about fifty large lots.

No one invites me in for oysters and champagne so, after paddling slowly along the north and west shorelines, I pass over to Twin Islands instead.

This rocky pair, joined by the narrowest of causeways, were originally known as the Ulloa Islands, another reference to Hernán (or Hernando) Cortés, who won the battle of San Juan de Ulloa. In 1971 they were owned by Prince Philip's nephew, Prince Markgraf Max von Baden. Queen Elizabeth herself spent a day here during her royal tour on the yacht *Britannia*. She didn't have to rough it; there's a spacious log cabin–style lodge on the property, with big living and dining rooms, seven bedrooms and five bathrooms.

When the next owner of the property began a clear-cutting operation, tremors of outrage spread through the local community and far afield. Now the islands have changed hands once again, the latest purchasers preferring their rocks forested rather than scalped. Falling has ceased and a vigilant peace has returned to the region.

Back at Hollyhock we settle easily into the retreat centre's soothing rhythms. Comfortable, woodsy rooms and cabins are scattered throughout the forested property, connected by footpaths to the main lodge and to smaller session and meditation spaces, many of which are beautifully designed. A store offers art, jewelry, journals, books, CDs, videos and local crafts. While classes are in session I stroll the grounds, read or work from my laptop on the lodge's airy deck. Then the mealtime bell rings again, hurray, and we all get another chance to visit the gourmet buffet, with its vegetarian curries, pastas, casseroles, quiches, soups, salads, fresh-baked goods and fab fruit and dairy desserts.

Hollyhock's programs leave plenty of free time, and during one interlude Katherine and I paddle south from the resort to the tip of Cortes at Sutil Point. The southern portions of the island (along with Hernando, Marina and Savary) are flat drifts of sand, gravel, rocks and boulders deposited when the great glaciers that carved out the Strait of Georgia melted. Wonderful beaches can be found along these gentle shores, but the boulders, many of which lurk offshore just beneath the water's surface, make racing around in powerboats a sport for the unwary.

Another sunny afternoon we transport the kayaks to Mansons Lagoon, part of a provincial marine park. Cortes has a number of these enticing tidal zones: shallow, lake-like expanses of saltwater that drain into the sea via narrow entrances. Without adequate flushing, such bayous can get scummy and lifeless, but Mansons ebbs and floods like a lung, and we play with our vessels on its warm, crystalline currents, gaping at the solid underlay of oysters, sand dollars, mussels and crabs. Other lagoons on Cortes empty into Carrington Bay, Von Donop Inlet and Squirrel Cove.

From Mansons we paddle to a forbidding, high-walled portal called the Gorge, which opens into Gorge Harbour, a favourite anchorage for yachts, full of tiny coves and alluring islets. Halfway up one of the Gorge's cliff faces, tiny figurative pictographs in red ochre guard the entrance and remind travellers of the area's first residents. According to legend, they hurled huge rocks down from the clifftops at unwanted visitors.

Arriving back at the retreat centre, a pleasing aroma reaches us—and a joyful sound. Can it be fresh oysters roasting at beachside and cheerful Hollyhockers celebrating with drum and flute? It is. With grateful sighs, we sink back one more night onto the resort's restorative, restful bosom.

Life on Cortes, needless to say, is not all singing and dancing. Much energy is also expended on the ubiquitous question of natural resource use, and here the going is not always smooth. The main issue currently facing islanders is the ongoing sale by US forestry giant Weyerhaeuser of its private land holdings in central Cortes, some of which, as we see when we drive along Gorge Harbour Road, are being bought and clear-cut by smaller logging companies.

The goal of the Cortes Ecoforestry Society is to incorporate these and other public lands into a community-managed forest. In both size and scope, the society's project would amount to one of the most significant sustainable-forestry models ever created in the province. The idea, and it's not a new one—though few examples exist in BC despite years of effort and a supposedly supportive government—is to develop practices that preserve functional ecosystems, promote the rural economy, respect diverse forest values, support eco-certification and establish markets for value-added "green" products. BC's Ministry of Forests announced recently that it was planning to grant between ten and thirty new community forest licences.

Many other conservation groups are active on Cortes. The island is home, for instance, to the *Watershed Sentinel*, one of BC's best-known environmental magazines. When publisher and editor Delores Broten and her partner, associate editor Don Malcolm, started out in 1990, the *Sentinel* was only distributed on Cortes and Quadra. "I had no intention of becoming involved in all this environmental activity when I first arrived here," explains Broten. "We were just looking for a place to live at the end of the road." Now her periodical is available—on 100 percent post-consumer recycled, chlorine-free newsprint, of course—Canada-wide. The periodical's print run has grown from 250 to 8,000, its size from sixteen to thirty-two pages. More than 12,000 people read each of its six free annual issues; a companion website gets about 25,000 visits a month (*www.watershedsentinel.ca*).

As its name suggests, the publication keeps watch and alerts readers about a welter of environmental concerns. The focus is largely on BC, though almost a quarter of the articles deal with Canadian or international topics relevant to BC residents. According to its publisher, the *Sentinel's* most important stories include a series about saving the Nechako River salmon from Alcan's power turbines and a piece about BC's biggest chlorine accident at a Powell River pulp mill. "We really couldn't have done all this without the community supporting us," she says. "In a way, we're like the island's megaphone out into the world."

Then there's FOCI, the Friends of Cortes Island. FOCI, which originally started up the *Watershed Sentinel*, deals with a wide range of complex issues, as well, but they all have to do with the current and future growth of Cortes itself. Drinking water, sewage disposal, community development, transportation, tourism and recreation, housing, government services—these thorny topics and more are of intense interest to FOCI supporters.

Katherine and I benefit from FOCI's efforts directly when we go hiking in Kw'as Park, a seventy-hectare forested area between Hague and Gunflint lakes, close to Mansons Landing. The park's excellent trail system was developed by FOCI's parks committee, led by Pierre de Trey. We enter from the north, off Seaford Road, and are soon swallowed up in a fresh-scented world of spruce trees and veteran Douglas-firs. To our delight, among the delicate herbs unfurling new leaves beside the paths we find hundreds of shoots of western coralroot, a bright purple orchid. A saprophyte, it dispenses with such plant basics as green foliage, chlorophyll and photosynthesis, preferring to dine directly on decayed organic matter.

The well-signed trails proceed in a series of loops so that you can spend hours there and rarely have to retrace your steps. We work our way to the remains of an old donkey or steam winch, left over from logging days in the 1920s. This industrial debris has a sad story attached; somehow the donkey's boiler overheated and exploded, scalding the engineer, Harry Hazel, so severely that the poor fellow died en route to hospital only a week before he had been planning to get married.

We are impressed enough with Kw'as Park that we come back another day, starting at the southern entrance, near Bartholomew Road, and hike along a ridge of big redcedars, cross the bridge between the two lakes and explore the eastern shoreline of Gunflint Lake. From here we have a fine view of yet another Cortes institution: Linnaea Farm, 130 hectares of agricultural and forest land protected by conservation covenants and dedicated to organic gardening, selective harvesting and public education. The farm's trail system is open to the public and connects with the one in Kw'as Park. Linnaea offers an eight-month residental gardening program for those interested in alternative food production, marketing and horticulture techniques. It also runs a potato co-op, sells seeds and produce from its garden stand, and operates the independent Linnaea School, which provides a rich learning experience for sixty children from kindergarten age to grade eight.

Everywhere we've ventured so far has been on the southern half of Cortes. There are good reasons for this, of course: that's where the roads and the people are, and it's the prettiest, driest part of the island. But there's another whole aspect to Cortes that we haven't seen. And the only way we can really view it is from the water.

Early one morning we drive just north of Whaletown to Coulter Bay on the west side of the island, the end of the public road system, and launch our kayaks. As we load up, an oyster farmer transfers his produce, packed in net bags, from the float to a pickup truck. It's calm as we paddle north and cross the wide mouth of Carrington Bay, where we glimpse three harbour porpoises.

After two hours we find some disturbed, choppy water and the nearly hidden entrance to Von Donop Inlet. Soon we're safely inside. Von Donop, 5.5 kilometres long and very narrow, named after a Royal Navy midshipman stationed at Esquimalt in the 1860s, almost bisects the mountainous, uninhabited northern part of Cortes. Practically the entire inlet is protected as part of 1,277-hectare Ha'thayim Provincial Marine Park, a popular place for boaters in summer. About two kilometres in we find a rustic campsite with an old picnic table and set up our tent on a soft bed of leaf litter beneath massive, ancient red cedars.

We come across a deer carcass, picked clean by rodents, reminding us that Cortes is still home to a few wolves and cougars. A faint trail leads to a nearby set of rapids, about 200 metres long, that drain Von Donop's large saltwater lagoon. As with Mansons Lagoon the current has fostered extravagant marine life, but here the mix is different: a carpet of green and pink sea anemones, purple sea stars, red and yellow bat stars. Red rock crabs and big spider crabs crawl over dense, colourful mats of seaweed.

By eight p.m. the tide has risen. Now the lagoon entrance is deep enough, and the current weak enough, that we can nose

LATE AFTERNOON OYSTER ROAST AND DRUM SESSION AT HOLLYHOCK

our kayaks into its torrent. This liquid bottleneck connecting lagoon to inlet is, in fact, a set of reversing rapids, and as it approaches equilibrium, it's fun to paddle against the dying outflow, then burst through into the lagoon, then shoot back out, all the while dodging rocks. On the lagoon side, masses of small fish are schooled, waiting for the day's supply of ocean nutrients to be delivered by the incoming tide. A kingfisher hovers and dives, while a stern bald eagle perches on a rock to watch our antics.

That night the weather changes; in the morning we're greeted by overcast skies and light drizzle—not unpleasant conditions to paddle in if you have adequate clothing. We set out after breakfast to explore Von Donop. Starting with the hand loggers of the 1880s, there's been plenty of wood cut over the decades. From the 1920s to the 1950s, several families

HOLLYHOCK'S TRADEMARK FLOWERS LINE THE ENTRANCE TO THE RESORT'S WONDERFUL ORGANIC GARDEN.

lived here on floathomes and operated a logging camp. There were enough children to establish a school. Settlers also lived at the head of the lagoon, raising rabbits for fur and meat. There's little sign now, though, of human presence. Most shorelines have returned to a natural state.

We pass other picnic tables on our rounds but don't see a better camp than the one we already have. At the inlet's deepest point a well-used trail, clearly marked, leads through groves of alder to Squirrel Cove on the far side of Cortes. It's only one kilometre long, level enough for portaging, and makes a pleasant walk and break from paddling. Squirrel Cove, with little bays and islands and its own saltwater lagoon, would also be a good destination for kayakers.

When we get back to Von Donop we pick up a good trail that seems to run right round the head of the inlet. We follow it for several kilometres, hoping it will lead us to the site of the old Von Donop community, but eventually give up and return to our boats. Apparently a decrepit cabin was used as the school until 1950, at which time a visiting inspector condemned it as "hazardous to life," and a replacement building was floated in. By 1952 there weren't enough children to sustain the school and it closed.

That evening, back at camp, the drizzle turns into a steady, relentless downpour, but we keep dry enough under our giant cedars and a large tarp. Camping in the rain is confining; you want to avoid getting your clothing and gear too wet because you don't know when you'll be able to dry it out again, but everything ends up feeling damp anyway. We read and snack and watch the light fall in the entrance to the inlet, wondering all the while if we'll get out next morning.

At five a.m. it's still raining. We break camp, dismantling the tent and packing our bags under the tarp in order to remain dry. The inlet is calm but once outside we're faced with rough water all the way back. At Carrington, where we see a porpoise again, we dare not cross the open mouth and, instead, paddle deep into the bay and behind Jane Islet to take advantage of calmer water. The final stretch, into Coulter Bay, is a grind, with headwinds and steepening waves, but we've handled worse. Thoughts of hot meals and dry clothes impel us back to our launch site. Next thing we know the truck is in the ferry lineup and we're draining large coffees at a store named Whaletown Widgets.

The ferry from Whaletown on Cortes to Heriot Bay on Quadra is the *Tenaka*, and it only holds thirty vehicles. We are vehicle number thirty-two. Oh, well, only another two-hour wait. Now, at least, the sun comes out. But we wonder about the ferry: if it's fully utilized on a Wednesday morning in

May, what must the situation be like on a Sunday evening in August? Tourists beware. But perhaps islanders prefer it this way—not long waits, of course, but the fact that only a limited number of vehicles can crowd their way onto Cortes. A larger vessel would only lead to faster growth.

Gilean Douglas, the island's conscience, wrote a book about her life on Cortes called *The Protected Place*, published in 1979. It's a paean to the powers of nature and to Cortes as "the promised land" in which she could become one with the spirit of the wilderness. But Douglas was a politician and planner as well as a poet, and she served for years as the island's elected director on the Comox-Strathcona regional district board. She was well aware that the beauty of Cortes was "its greatest asset," and she helped put into place many policies and bylaws to conserve that beauty. The number one goal in the island's official community plan, last revised in 1995, is "to preserve the rural quality of the area while protecting its ecological integrity."

Despite the fact that Douglas was starting "to feel like a stranger" way back in 1971, her efforts have not been in vain. Managing future growth is certainly a central concern for everyone we meet and talk to. Typical of the comments we hear are those of ten-year resident Dianne Bersea, the artist we'd encountered back at Mansons Landing Community Hall. "Cortes," she says, "is small enough and isolated enough that, ten months of the year, you know everyone you see. And I like that."

LAX KW'ALAAMS FROM ROSE ISLAND,
WITH GRACE CHURCH DOMINATING THE SCENE

Lax Kw'alaams

New links to the world for old Port Simpson

As we walk along the beach we keep our eyes to the ground, searching for the blue glass trade beads that wash up on occasion in front of Lax Kw'alaams. All we find among the shell fragments and polished stones are shards of glass and crockery and nubs of corroded metal. Still, these give us a sniff of the past. The beads, though, are from a time when this community was known as Fort Simpson. In those days the shore would have been lined with cedar lodges and canoes and loomed over by the tall, red-trimmed pickets of a Hudson's Bay Company stockade. Outside these walls more than 2,000 individuals—a restless, noisy, ever-changing population—convened to trade furs and other goods and services for blankets, clothing, guns, tobacco and alcohol. The beads, known as *somentaskins*, or "little gifts," were thrown in as a bonus after a good session of bartering.

Today Lax Kw'alaams, located 40 kilometres north of Prince Rupert and 775 kilometres from Vancouver, is a placid First Nation village of about 1,200 souls. No signs remain of the fort, and few would guess that, north of Oregon, this was once the most important outpost of the British Empire on the west coast of North America. Wooden boats, tipped on their sides at the water's edge, quietly decay. Tsimshian mothers push baby strollers, and pickups trundle by. Most people make their livelihood from fishing these days, and numerous gillnetters and trollers are docked in the fine harbour. Houses perch beside unpaved streets that spread in haphazard fashion up the slope from the ocean. The red-roofed steeple of Grace United Church dominates the scene.

Eddie Knott has alerted us to the possible presence of the trade beads on the beach. He and his wife, Karen, operate Knott's Landing, the cozy bed and breakfast where we're staying. Eddie, who also owns the *Lady Mellissa*, an eleven-metre gillnetter, has just returned from fishing one of the season's first sockeye openings, and he's giving us a quick rundown of things to do and see at Lax Kw'alaams. His list is not a long one.

Most visitors to the village are there for outdoor recreational activities or else they're working. Our fellow guests at Knott's Landing include a mechanic from Prince Rupert, a health-care worker from Prince George and a couple from Kelowna who travel around BC offering photographic services. For a fee they'll do portraits of the kids or put your mug on a coffee cup. Visitors from as far away as England and Florida have signed the guestbook, and many praise the sport fishing, kayaking and friendliness of the villagers, especially Karen and Eddie.

Lax Kw'alaams, without a doubt, has one of the most spectacular histories of any community in the province, though few tourists come to breathe in the past. It's there, right on the main street, outside the tribal council office and near where the trading post once stood. A few well-worn gravestones, broken and uncared for, commemorate important nineteenth-century figures: Abraham Lincoln, chief of the Kitsheese tribe, "died July 21, 1890, aged 85 years"; Paul Skagwait, "third chief, died May 23, 1887, aged 40 years." One memorial celebrates Legaic, "first head chief"—a legendary, powerful Tsimshian leader who controlled much of the region's fur trade during the early days of the fort—and his descendants, who also took the name Legaic (or Ligeex).

The Hudson's Bay Company first set up shop in the area in 1831, on Nass Bay, sixty kilometres farther north. The site was chosen by Aemilius Simpson, commander of the *Cadboro*, an HBC vessel; when he died there later that year it was renamed in his honour. Fort Nass, as it was initially called, was poorly located and almost inaccessible in winter. In 1834 the post was moved to its present location, a traditional camping ground of Chief Legaic, whose status and power were thereby enhanced. Another Fort Simpson, in the Northwest Territories, honours George Simpson, illustrious former governor of the HBC, which created confusion. The name was changed again at century's end, to Port Simpson, which reduced but did not eliminate the chance that mail would be delayed for months as it made a 1,900-kilometre diversion to the frozen banks of the Liard River.

While the Tsimshian people have always known this spot as Lax Kw'alaams, or "place of wild roses," that name proved difficult for non-Native speakers. The post office didn't adopt it until 1998. I've seen many spelling variations: Lochgwaahlamsh, Laxtgu'alaams, Larhkwaralamps. But the name does explain why the small island that is home to the oldest part of the

TSIMSHIAN BEAR DESIGN ON LONGHOUSE
OPPOSITE LAX KW'ALAAMS ADMINISTRATION BUILDING

community, known on some maps as Village Island, is more commonly referred to as Rose Island. And indeed, the huge, sweet-scented blossoms of the Nootka rose, along with cow parsnip and sea-watch, or angelica, are everywhere when we visit in June.

Eddie recommends that we cross the bridge that connects Rose Island to the mainland and explore a new boardwalk that the villagers have built, and this quickly becomes one of our favourite activities. The fine wooden promenade encircles an early burial site on the far side of the island, out of the community's view and facing the ocean. This is sacred ground. The forest is dense and old, with groves of unusual hemlock trees, their trunks weathered into uneven, corrugated shapes. Benches invite you to linger, and steps lead down to a pretty beach, where raucous raven and bald eagle families jockey loudly for control. "That boardwalk really brought back a lot of memories for people," Eddie tells us. "Hardly any of the coastal villages have them any more."

Elsewhere in Lax Kw'alaams the walking is not so pleasant. This is because all the streets in town are being torn up in preparation for paving, a project expected to take four years. The dust is ferocious. One of the reasons the project is being undertaken, ironically, is to control the dust. Of course, if you're going to dig up the roads, you might as well fix the curbs and sidewalks, too, and upgrade water and sewer lines at the same time. The end result will be a huge improvement, no doubt, but in the meantime everyone's patience is being tested.

Another major road project is completed, fortunately, just before we arrive. The eighteen-kilometre route to the ferry terminal at the head of protected Tuck Inlet, once a hideous drive that took an hour to complete, has had $8 million thrown at it and is now a smooth, painless twenty-minute spin. The ferry itself, the fifteen-vehicle *Spirit of Lax Kw'alaams*, formerly the *Nicola* and leased from BC Ferries, takes about an hour to reach Prince Rupert. This service started in 1997 and has been a boon for the community. Before then you had to fly into the village, an expensive way to go grocery shopping, or else take a small water taxi that only braved the often-rough winter waters of Chatham Sound several times a week. "Sometimes," explains Karen Knott, "you were almost risking your life by taking that 'outside' route."

These problems, of course, pale beside the risks experienced by the inhabitants of early Fort Simpson. From behind their whitewashed stockade, the twenty or so fort employees looked out on a wild and often dangerous scene. Disagreements and skirmishes between hostile First Nations groups were frequent, sometimes resulting in extended gun battles and serious loss of life. Disease and hunger were endemic, as was drunkenness on both sides of the stockade; even after the HBC stopped selling liquor, in the 1840s, renegade rum traders caused havoc with the local tribes. Sometimes the fort itself was attacked, or pickets torn down and carried off, or the palisade set on fire. The traders mounted eight small cannons on two corner bastions, mostly for show, but these were fired in earnest from time to time. Ammunition was scarce; the factor would pay a shilling for each cannon ball brought back to be fired again.

The unruly godlessness of the community did not escape zealous missionary eyes. Anglican William Duncan lived at Fort Simpson for four years before establishing his famed Christian utopia at Metlakatla, twenty-five kilometres to the south. Thomas Crosby, a Methodist, arrived in 1874 and built an enormous monument, Grace Church, to compete with St. Paul's, the thousand-seater Duncan had erected at Metlakatla. Both temples succumbed to fire, St. Paul's in 1901 and Grace in 1931. Only the latter was reconstructed.

Despite all the dangers and inconveniences, Fort Simpson was a success. It did a valuable trade, not only in furs but also in whale, dogfish and seal oil, whale bone, woven hats and mats, stone pipes, bear gall bladders and beaver musk glands. Gradually, though, business declined. After Prince Rupert was founded in 1906 as the terminus of the Grand Trunk Pacific Railway, speculators tried to flog house lots in Port Simpson, claiming that the glorious future assuredly ahead for the railway town must surely extend to its northern neighbour. But such wasn't the case.

The fort's palisade and bastions came down in the 1880s. The trading post itself burned to the ground in 1914. It was not rebuilt, though the HBC did run a store in Port Simpson from 1934 to 1954. Today the most prominent structure in town is a controversial fish cannery, built in 1975 with provincial funding over the objections of the federal government and private companies, which claimed that it represented subsidized and unfair competition. The plant started life as a First Nations co-op, but changed hands several times over the years and is now being renovated by a Japanese company.

Today a slew of new buildings is rising in Lax Kw'alaams, including a seniors' housing project and a fine recreation centre. Karen Knott hopes the centre will have a strong cultural element, with some facilities—a café, perhaps, a small museum—that might attract more tourists to her town. In their attempts to create jobs and build a viable local economy, community leaders have focused their energies mostly on fishing and forestry. Karen and Eddie feel that tourism could become a strong third component to the mix and a way to capture at least a small fraction of Lax Kw'alaams' extraordinary past.

POWELL RIVER'S FORMER PROVINCIAL BUILDING HAS BEEN CONVERTED INTO AN APPEALING HOSTEL AND RESTAURANT.

On the Malaspina

Powell River and Lund struggle to diversify

Passing through Powell River a few years ago, en route to Comox and northern Vancouver Island, I zipped into the offices of the *Powell River Peak*, the local newspaper, and dropped off a copy of my latest book. I was hoping that someone would interview me or write a review, and as I waited to speak to an editorial staffer I leafed through the current copy of the *Peak*. There I was flabbergasted to discover an article accusing me of injuring the town's reputation. "Writer raises a stink," read the headline. The story went on to tear a strip off me for a piece I'd written about Powell River in *Vancouver* magazine the month before. This wasn't the kind of publicity I had in mind.

My article had been part of a benign "ten great summer escapes" medley, and I'd focused on Powell River's old townsite—Canada's only National Historic District outside the

Maritimes—saying what a pleasant place it was to wander around. I didn't write the piece to please the town, but I did feel that residents, especially those in charge of tourism, might be pleased with it. Vancouver is Powell River's main market for potential visitors, and here was a story, in a prominent Vancouver publication, extolling the town's appeal—or so I'd thought.

But people were not pleased. Not at all. The president of the visitors' bureau was quoted as saying she'd become "angry" when she read my article. The manager of another civic organization thought the piece was "damaging to the community." The mayor thundered—somewhat ominously, I felt—that he'd like to "broaden [my] horizon and appreciation of what really Powell River is all about." What on earth had I done?

I'd committed a cardinal sin. I had "reinforced the community's image as a milltown" by writing that the townsite was built around a "smoke-snorting" industrial operation—one of BC's oldest and largest pulp and paper mills, now owned by NorskeCanada. Then, to make matters worse, I'd perpetrated the ultimate taboo, mentioning that the mill effluent sometimes smelled like rotten eggs. Ouch! It didn't matter, apparently, that I'd also described the great hiking near Powell River, the world-class canoe circuit, the sea-kayaking opportunities, the excellent restaurants and accommodation, and the Sliammon First Nation's fascinating cultural tours. The only thing that local officials picked up on (and the only thing covered by the newspaper) was the fact that I'd been rude enough to mention the mill.

Powell River is many things, of course, but whether or not people want to admit it, its reason for existence is still the pulp and paper plant. In the 1910s and '20s, a quintessential company town grew up around the mill. The Powell River Co. had complete control over the community and its workers' lives. By the standards of the time, it treated them well, providing low-cost housing, electricity, heat, a hospital, stores, landscaping and some of the best recreational facilities anywhere.

In 1930, the commercial centre moved two kilometres south, out of sight (and smell) of the mill, to Westview, where it is today. Few new structures were raised in the old section, resulting in a movie-set townscape fixed in '20s amber. There are some fine old buildings: a mock-Tudor bank; a handsome hostel that used to be the provincial building; several attractive churches; stately homes on Manager's Row; unusual apartment blocks, one of which was formerly the hospital; a beautiful community hall; the 1911 Rodmay Hotel (named after early proprietors Rod and May MacIntyre); and the Patricia Theatre, BC's oldest operating movie house.

Walking maps of the old town are available, and in summer there are often free tours. Many homes are still proudly maintained by long-time millworkers. In fact, while researching my *Vancouver* article, eighty-nine-year-old Nathan Clark materialized beside me, invited me into his immaculate dwelling and showed me the plaque the district had awarded him for his preservation efforts. Everyone I met in the townsite was friendly and welcoming. But as you're walking round, it's pretty hard to miss the mill itself, with its gigantic smokestack. I couldn't have pretended it didn't exist.

So I mentioned the dreaded "M" word and inadvertently became an Enemy of the Town. After reading about the stink I'd raised, I met *Peak* editor Laura Walz and tried to convey my astonishment at how I'd been treated. Two weeks later another, shorter article appeared, this one entitled "Scribe likes town's charms," in which I attempted to persuade Powell River that being a milltown was not necessarily a stigma, especially if you were also a National Historic District. No need to be defensive, I pleaded. Perhaps history and architecture buffs will visit as well as ecotourists.

I report this incident to forewarn innocent readers, should they visit Powell River, not to give offence by making politically incorrect remarks. In truth, the town and its surrounding areas suffer from a kind of split personality. For decades the economy of the region has been dominated by one industry: forestry. That industry's fortunes are now in decline. More economic diversification is desperately needed, especially in the tourism sector, which has vast potential. Unfortunately, historic ties between the town, the mill and the logging companies have been so tight for so long that they're throttling the community's ability to change. Old attitudes still rule the roost; even the region's official tourism boosters, while happy to berate a visiting reporter, fall silent whenever the needs of a diversified economy conflict with the desires of the forest industry.

Nowhere is this dichotomy more pronounced than on the Malaspina Peninsula north of Powell River, which juts off from the BC mainland like a hitchhiker's thumb. Malaspina beckons toward the wilderness at the north end of the Strait of Georgia, which it has more in common with than the forestry-dependent stretch of coastline it is actually attached to. This is as far as you can drive on BC's mainland coast. It's the end of the road, but also the jumping-off spot for Desolation Sound Provincial Marine Park and a paradise of islands: Savary, Hernando, Cortes and the Redondas.

The peninsula is a saving grace of recreational wealth. Malaspina and Okeover Arm provincial parks occupy more than half its eastern shoreline. Copeland Islands Provincial Marine Park, just off the west coast, attracts paddlers (as do all the nearby waters). The Sunshine Coast Trail and branches of the Greenways trail system offer hiking experiences as rich as any in BC. And the attractive little waterfront village of Lund is a Mecca for boaters and fishers and scuba divers. Sadly, the government is not working overtime to preserve the area's natural beauty and help low-impact tourism flourish in order to offset the forestry downturn.

Malaspina residents have mounted a spirited recent campaign to protect certain natural amenities from an unprecedented assault. The main focus of local concerns is a small but beautiful campground near Dinner Rock, one of more than fifteen recreational sites in the region that have long been operated by BC's Ministry of Forests, but which government now wishes to rid itself of. The cost and bother of maintaining these campsites is no longer considered to be in the public interest. Dinner Rock was also threatened by a major logging operation, which would harvest trees right up to the edge of the campground.

I'd pitched my tent at this spot—right on the coast, with fine views across the water to Savary Island—on numerous occasions. A plaque commemorates a tragic event that occurred just offshore, on Dinner Rock itself, where the coastal steamer MV *Gulf Stream* ran aground and turned on its side in 1947, causing the deaths of five passengers, including three children. The incident took place on a dark, rainy night in October, while the vessel was on its way to Lund with forty-one passengers and crew. From the campsite you can just make out a white cross atop Dinner Rock. It was helicoptered into place in 1998, half a century after Henry Pavid, whose eighteen-month-old daughter Jean lost her life in the accident, had erected an original cross, now in the Powell River Museum.

The Ministry of Forests had asked the Powell River Regional District if it was interested in taking over the operation of several forest recreation sites, including Dinner Rock. But district directors, supposedly desperate to promote tourism in their area, voted unanimously against the idea, claiming that no funds were available for maintenance and that it was the province's responsibility, anyway, to look after such facilities.

Neither the ministry, the district nor the forest industry showed any interest in preserving a network of trails in the Dinner Rock area. Some of them, such as the delightful, wheelchair-accessible Brown Creek Trail, which had actually been built with public funds and forest industry support, were slated to be clear-cut, without even the visual respite of a buffer zone of trees.

The nearby Atrevida Loop Trail was also afflicted by a clear-cut logging proposal, despite the fact that it supported exactly the kind of innovative business the region is anxious to attract. Lori Kemp, who has since sold up and moved to Vancouver Island, offered "goatpacking" services at her guest-house, Hiker's Haven, whereby people with limited mobility (and anyone else) could hike the Loop while Kemp's trained goats carried their loads. "Visitors do not come to hike into clear-cuts," she declared sadly.

The efforts of local people did eventually have some effects; in several areas, including Dinner Rock, cutblocks have been removed from current logging plans (though they can be reintroduced in the future). And a new and more progressive representative from the area was elected to the district board. "But what we really need here," insists Patricia Keays, a director of the Eco-Care Conservancy of the Powell River Region, which spearheaded the Malaspina campaign, "is a land-use plan that takes into account *all* the values of the forest resource, not just the timber values."

The tiny community of Lund, northern terminus of a coastal highway system that stretches to Puerto Montt in Chile, is the soul of the Malaspina Peninsula. It's also one of my favourite local destinations. Two ferry rides and 150 kilometres north-west of Vancouver, it's a quiet spot in winter, home to a handful of prawners and other fisher folk. But it livens up in July and August. Water taxis run a regular service to nearby Savary Island, where white sands and aquamarine waters are the lure. Thousands of pleasure boaters and kayakers pass through Lund's small harbour, heading for Desolation Sound and beyond. Cafés and a bakery (with great blackberry cinnamon buns) cater to the transient throng. And presiding over all this laid-back bustle is the 1895 Lund Hotel, a historic coast landmark with its steep roofline, dormer windows and wrap-around second-floor veranda.

The hotel, once known as the Malaspina, was built by Lund's founders, Fred and Charles Thulin. It's the heart of the hamlet, site of a general store, post office and pub. But it had seen better days. By 1999, when the property came up for sale after its last owner had gone bankrupt, it was rundown and ripe for dismantling. Fortunately it caught the eye of two local investors—a Powell River businessman and the Sliammon First Nation—who joined forces to buy and renovate the old structure. The newly refurbished rooms are simple but comfortable, with sensational views. And the restyled

Above: BRACKEN FERNS IN AUTUMN

Below: ONE OF POWELL RIVER'S MANY TRAILS LEADS FROM POWELL LAKE TO WILDWOOD HEIGHTS.

restaurant and oceanside pub, complete with outdoor patio, have been resoundingly embraced by locals and tourists alike.

Katherine and I drive up to Lund for the hotel's grand opening. The genial new owners are hosting a celebration, and the staff of Ayjoomixw Tours, a Sliammon ecotourism company, have arranged for native dancers to perform. Salmon is being barbecued over an open fire and then served to visitors along with salmonberries and bannock. Later, a 9.5-metre fibreglass replica dugout canoe will be launched in the cove beside the hotel and paddled round the harbour by groups of eager hotel patrons.

The next day we have a chance to travel in this vessel ourselves. Seven of us, including Murray Mitchell, or Tlex-tan, our First Nation guide, surf a strong southeasterly through Thulin Passage and the Copelands and into Malaspina Inlet. Even though the waves are steep, especially around Sarah Point, I feel perfectly safe in this giant canoe, which is wonderfully fast and stable in a following sea.

By noon we've worked up quite an appetite, so we stop for a generous lunch of grilled salmon and assorted salads. Tlex-tan, a skilled carver, grew up on Cortes Island and tells us stories while we eat. The weather has become so windy that, back at Lund, concerned employees have asked the Coast Guard to check on us. A Zodiac is dispatched and two survival-suited officers soon find us on our beach, happily gorging ourselves on salmon, without a care in the world. Thus reassured, they head back and we continue down Malaspina Inlet, struggling against the wind now, and end our journey in heavy rain at the head of Trevenen Bay, where we're met by car and returned to Lund. We are exhilarated by the ride, even in this wild weather; on a fine day the trip would be pure heaven.

Back at the hotel, I talk to manager Steve Tipton, who supervised the million-dollar restoration. "The place was in horrible shape after years of neglect," he says. Everything had to be upgraded, from the foundations to the beams to the roof. A complete new kitchen was installed, new store facilities, new plumbing, new furnishings—you name it. Twenty rooms in a more modern annex to the old hotel were readied first, along with the restaurant and pub. Phase two will see twenty more luxurious rooms and suites completed on the second and third floors of the original building.

Dave Formosa, who owns the successful Shinglemill bistro, pub and marina on Powell Lake, is the local businessman providing the management expertise and 49 percent of the funding. The rest of the money and a large portion of enthusiasm come from the Sliammon Development Corporation, business arm of the 850-strong Sliammon First Nation, whose main village is located between Lund and Powell River.

The opening of the hotel is a homecoming of sorts for the Sliammon people, who lived at Lund for centuries before the Thulin brothers decided to settle there. L. Maynard Harry, chief of the Sliammon council and a director of the development corporation, believes that economic initiatives such as the hotel renovation can do more than provide jobs for his people. "It creates a feeling of pride," he says. "It's the first time we've explored this kind of opportunity. The whole community of Sliammon is very excited about the project." And Lund is thrilled, too: "Everyone supports rebuilding the hotel," one resident tells me. "We got our town back."

I've been through Powell River many times since my literary fall from grace. No one has yet attempted to broaden my horizon, though I keep my head down, just in case. The town, pinched between Malaspina Strait and the expanse of Powell Lake, forms a kind of bottleneck, and you must pass through it in order to get farther north on the coast or take a ferry over to Texada Island or Comox. Sometimes, though, I come just to visit Powell River; after all, with a population of about 15,000, this is the largest community on the mainland coast between Vancouver and Prince Rupert.

The town grows on you, I find. Westview, with its Georgia Strait panorama and busy waterfront, has a funky main street of small shops and cafés. Exquisite bird images formed with multicoloured strips of metal have been embedded right into the sidewalks. For a change of pace, I might drive round the suburb of Cranberry Lake or else visit the fine little museum and walk on Willingdon Beach. If there's time, lunch at the Shinglemill is definitely in order.

I've hardly begun to tap the recreational opportunities in the surrounding area, where an array of outdoor options exist that most small cities can only dream about. Because the original mill owners needed to attract employees to their remote operation—and wanted workers who would stick around, preferably married men with families—they helped develop everything from baseball diamonds to lawn bowling greens. Civic leaders added to the bounty over the years. Today, besides serving the townspeople, these amenities attract visitors from far and wide.

There is, for starters, the Powell Forest Canoe Route, a semicircular itinerary that connects twelve lakes via a series of well-built portages and can cover from 57 to over 150 kilometres, depending on your route. The portage sections have resting racks conveniently spaced at five-minute intervals; twenty campsites, most accessible only by foot and paddle, are scattered along the way.

For hikers, the Sunshine Coast Trail extends north from Saltery Bay to the tip of the Malaspina Peninsula at Sarah Point. It can be trekked as a 180-kilometre multi-day slog or broken into up to twenty-seven different self-contained day trips. The route features dozens of spectacular viewpoints and has been designed to connect some of the upper Sunshine Coast's rapidly vanishing pockets of old-growth forest. Numerous campsites have been built, many with picnic tables and toilets, and more are planned for the future, along with cabins for hut-to-hut hiking.

Ocean kayaking, as I've mentioned, can take place, in style, almost anywhere in the region: along mainland shores, in Jervis Inlet and Desolation Sound, on dozens of large lakes, around hundreds of offshore islands. Scuba diving is popular too—on wrecks, with octopi, or to Canada's first underwater statue, a mermaid, off Saltery Bay Provincial Park. There's a fine golf course at Myrtle Point I'd like to try. And one of these days we really must cruise up Powell Lake to visit Fiddlehead Farm, an isolated homestead-style hostel set in mountain wilderness.

Soon, I hope, I'll be able to pass through Powell River with head held high. I encourage you to visit, too. Just don't mention the mill.

NAMU'S CREAKY BOARDWALK PASSES SEVERAL LARGE BUNKHOUSES DESIGNED FOR WORKERS WHO ARE SINGLE.

Disappearing Namu

A former fisheries centre moulders away

Namu is up for sale, I see, and has been for quite some time. On the LandQuest real-estate website the details are spelled out: eighty hectares of land, deepwater oceanfront, net loft, fish plant, ice plant, warehouses, marine ways, fuel tanks, docks. There are houses, a store, restaurant, office, standing timber and shoreline on beautiful Namu Lake. Just think of the possibilities. You could reactivate the fish-processing facility or build a cruise ship port or turn this former cannery site into a heritage park, which it richly deserves to be. "The best tourism and real-estate development potential on the BC coast," states the listing, with "fabulous fishing, kayaking, diving, wildlife viewing and petroglyphs."

A mere $1.25 million (reduced from $1.75 million) will buy the townsite, 450 kilometres northwest of Vancouver on the isolated central BC coast. It gets a bit wet up on Fitz Hugh

Sound, mind you, and the body of water Namu sits beside isn't called Whirlwind Bay for nothing. Namu itself, in fact, is a Heiltsuk First Nation word meaning "place of high winds." The homes are collapsing, the walkways disappearing under a green tsunami of bushes and weeds. But what a great resort this spot would make. It's already a living museum, drenched in coastal history. I'll bet you could get the whole place for less than the asking price.

I first saw Namu in 1996, from the deck of the *Queen of Chilliwack.* The abandoned town was a whistlestop on BC Ferries' Discovery Coast itinerary, but the *Queen* couldn't actually land there, as the docks were too dilapidated. This information came as a surprise to the middle-aged lady planning to join her husband's fishing boat. She hadn't realized she'd be jumping, in the grey light of early morning, from the ferry's car ramp to the rolling deck of a gillnetter.

A few years later I passed by again. By then a heavy-duty floating dock had been lashed in place at Namu, and the *Queen* nudged up to it and discharged a handful of kayakers and a horde of curious tourists. We could explore the townsite at our own risk, we were told—and please don't fall through the rotting boardwalks, which ran along the waterfront, through jungles of thimbleberry shrubs and out of town as far as the lake.

The industrial bits of Namu had been rebuilt after a disastrous fire and so are relatively intact. The blaze had apparently been started by a welder's torch as workers prepared for the opening of the herring season on a cold January day in 1962. The town's Heiltsuk name proved no exaggeration; strong winds whipped the flames into an instant holocaust and the main buildings were reduced to charred debris in a few hours. The power plant burnt, which caused the fire pumps to fail, leaving only a small fireboat to fight the inferno. The community's radio was destroyed, and no one knew the extent of the damage at first. Miraculously, none of the hundred or so people living at Namu at the time were injured.

The cannery was rebuilt but soon became obsolete, as fast packers with improved refrigeration facilities began transporting the bulk of the catch to Prince Rupert and Vancouver for processing. Namu cannery shut down for good in 1970 and the machinery was removed. But the town stayed alive as a supply and repair base for the central coast fishing fleet. Three concrete warehouses have been kept in good condition, and the store and café—when we were there, at least—looked as if they'd recently been in business. A diminutive truck in bright new red paint, proudly emblazoned with the initials of the Namu Fire Department, sat in the street with a load of handheld extinguishers.

Walking farther, carefully scanning the plank roads for signs of decay, we found an older Namu, one that had been set in motion by coastal pioneer Robert Draney. The Draney brothers, Robert and Thomas, arrived in BC from Ontario in the 1870s and helped build or manage canneries on the Skeena, in Rivers Inlet and at Bella Coola. In 1893 Robert Draney bought the Namu property from fur trader John Clayton, an even earlier pioneer, founded the Namu Canning Co. and constructed the original fish plant.

Later, as Namu prospered, Draney added a store and a sawmill; lumber was needed in the region for just about everything: docks, walkways, buildings and, especially, boxes to ship the cans of salmon. He rebuilt the cannery in 1911, installed electricity, then sold out in 1915 to R. V. Winch and Northern BC Fisheries Ltd. In 1923 Gosse-Millard acquired the operation; in 1928 BC Packers became the latest owner.

By the mid-1930s Namu was BC Packers' headquarters on the north coast. In 1936 the company added a reduction plant to produce meal and oil from fish wastes; the following year it greatly increased the size of the cannery; and in 1940 it erected a large cold-storage facility.

In the 1940s, the town was a busy little place. Its population of about 200 doubled as the fishing season approached. Namu even had districts. We pushed our way through the undergrowth to visit Shaughnessy Heights, where the single-family houses were newer and larger. The lower part of town was called Toonerville. Along the waterfront, large ramshackle bunkhouses once sheltered the single male workers, while the Japanese, Chinese and First Nations employees lived in separate, segregated areas.

The cannery could not have operated without its First Nations workers, who came from the main Heiltsuk community of Bella Bella, forty kilometres to the north on Campbell Island. Heiltsuk employees, especially women, washed fish; filled, cleaned, weighed and labelled cans; made and packed boxes; worked in the cold storage area; and mended nets. Girls as young as ten toiled at the cannery, assisting their mothers.

Although their jobs were hard and poorly paid, the female cannery employees did not view themselves as downtrodden and underprivileged, as some writers have portrayed them, but as a highly skilled and effective labour force. They took great pride in their work and, for the most part, enjoyed cannery life. The Heiltsuk women were prominent in the Native Sisterhood of BC, an assertive organization that negotiated with plant managers to improve housing, working conditions and pay for its members. The sudden closure of the cannery represented a blow to all its First Nations employees, saddening them and depriving them of an important source of income.

The history of the area goes much further back—10,000 years further, in fact—than the cannery era. Namu has the distinction of being one of the oldest recorded sites of human habitation on the BC coast and the longest regularly occupied site in Canada. The ancestors of the Heiltsuk people lived there, sometimes on a year-round basis, sometimes seasonally, and took full advantage of the ocean's rich resources. Over the centuries these occupants left behind heaping middens of shell, bone and other refuse that archaeologists first investigated in 1969.

Teams from Simon Fraser University (SFU) under Roy Carlson did much research at Namu in the 1970s, finding spear and harpoon heads, microblades (sharp stone chips used to make cutting tools), fish hooks, needles and many other artifacts. Some microblades were of obsidian that originated elsewhere in BC, and as far away as Oregon, and must have been brought to the central coast in trade. Complex burial sites were uncovered. A big cross-section of midden was painstakingly removed from a trench and transported to SFU to form a centrepiece at the Museum of Archaeology and Ethnology.

Before the archaeologists arrived, Namu's claim to fame, after canned salmon, was a killer whale. The animal was trapped offshore in fishing nets and confined in a small cove, then sold for $8,000 to Ted Griffin, a Seattle aquarium owner. Griffin built a special floating pen and, despite much scepticism, towed the orca all the way to Puget Sound without major problems. He trained it, and a Namu craze soon swept over North America. A movie was made. A rock song featured Namu's vocalizations. Next Griffin caught a female whale, Shamu, hoping the two would mate, but they did not, and Shamu was sold to Sea World in San Diego. After eleven months, Namu caught an infection from his pen's polluted waters and died. Griffin went on to help capture dozens of other animals to satisfy the unfortunate demand he had created for performing killer whales. In the process, the southern resident orca population lost an entire generation, throwing its survival into jeopardy.

Over the past decade the town of Namu has fallen into decrepitude. BC Packers sold it in 1991 to a private company whose owner planned to build a hotel and restaurant and turn the site into a tourist centre. Sadly, those plans proved too ambitious. The only sign of tourism we ever saw was the *Ocean Explorer I,* a floating fishing lodge operated by Chris Carlson, son of the archaeologist, which was based at Namu for several seasons.

Recently, even BC Ferries has cast Namu adrift. The *Queen of Chilliwack* no longer makes regular or request stops at the forlorn village of ghosts. With advance notice, kayakers can be lowered from the ferry, or "wet launched," in Whirlwind Bay, but for most passengers, a passing glimpse is all they'll ever get of this classic BC coastal community.

Unless you're reading chapters out of sequence, you will, by now, already have come across dozens of BC's nearly 7,000 islands. The "Cortes Culture" and "Sunny Savary" chapters, in particular, could easily have run in this section instead of the previous one. In BC, it seems, there's just no getting away from island life; nearly a quarter of the province's inhabitants reside on islands and have a deep familiarity with ferries.

The islands in these pages range in size from tiny to very large, but they all have something special going on. Some are being preserved as parks or by non-profit conservation groups. Others are in areas that are opening up more and more to tourism. At least one has the attention of scientists worldwide. These islands have character. They differ from their siblings and neighbours. Islands, by definition, are isolated from the mainland. You can't just drive away from them when you want to. They can be fragile and chaotic, but also intimate and comfortable. Often they are places where people gradually learn to accept and understand their true natures, and make homes for themselves on the wild, wet coast of British Columbia.

Islands Everywhere

ARRIVAL BY FERRY AT TEXADA ISLAND'S BLUBBER BAY TERMINAL

Texada's Sticklebacks

Mysterious evolution in the Strait of Georgia

Texada looms out of the Strait of Georgia like a fragment from a bad dream. Steep-sloped and dark-forested, with an inhospitable coastline and a relentless industrial past, the island can feel foreboding. A circumnavigation by kayak seems less than inviting (wasn't it here that a territorial seal made national headlines several years ago by attacking a paddler?), so we take the ferry over instead, from Powell River, for a stint of truck camping. At the Blubber Bay terminal on Texada's north end, all we can see is a huge limestone quarry, one of the biggest in BC. Well, at least they don't process whale blubber on these shores any longer.

When you leave the quarry behind, though, the views improve. Texada is the largest island in the strait, half again the size of Saltspring and over fifty kilometres long. At Van Anda, on the east coast, houses cling to the rocky slopes above

Sturt Bay, where an old, cracked lime kiln still stands. In the late nineteenth century, rich discoveries of gold and copper helped create a boomtown atmosphere, and Van Anda (named for Van Anda Blewett, son of a mining entrepreneur, and often spelled Vananda, even by the post office) soon sported hotels, a hospital, a smelter, a sawmill and, of all things, an opera house.

At the village of Gillies Bay, farther west, the tide recedes hundreds of metres to reveal great swaths of sand, ideal for July's Sandcastle Weekend. As the mines around Van Anda petered out in the 1950s, the iron-ore deposits near Gillies Bay, worked on and off since 1886, came into their heyday. Texada Mines employed hundreds here from 1952 until 1976, running underground and open-pit operations and shipping ore to Japan. Today, at both communities, retirees have taken over from miners; exotic gardens, complete with palm and banana trees, attest to the mild climate and an abundance of leisure time.

Like many places in BC, Texada is busy reinventing itself as a tourist destination. The island has a museum, a golf course, art galleries and craft studios; its attractions easily dispel the industrialized gloom that greets visitors when they first arrive. For campers, the regional park at Shelter Point, just south of Gillies Bay, is one of the nicest in BC, with terrific beaches and trails and its own fancy take-out, the Tree Frog Bistro. Farther south, at Shingle Beach's rustic, isolated Forest Service campsite, you can almost reach out and touch cruise ships passing through Sabine Channel.

Texada is also a naturalist's delight. Rare ferns and orchids flourish here (as do numerous illicit marijuana plants); rough-skin newts and painted turtles can be found. Certain lakes and

LITTLE BROWN FROGS TAKE THE SUN ON PRIEST LAKE'S FLOATING POND-LILY LEAVES.

streams, however, draw specialized biologists to the island in disproportionate droves. The most heavily studied body of water is Paxton Lake. Priest, Balkwill and Emily lakes—an interconnected group in the Vananda Creek watershed—have also received significant attention. Here, indeed, some of the planet's newest species are rapidly taking form. Who would have dreamed that quiet, unassuming Texada Island is a living laboratory of evolution?

The attraction is a tiny fish: the threespine stickleback. During the last ice age, when land levels rose and fell with the advance and decline of the glaciers, this common marine species managed to insinuate itself into numerous coastal lakes and streams and settle into a freshwater existence. In Paxton Lake and the Vananda Creek lakes (as well as in Enos Lake, near

THE BEACH AT SHELTER POINT REGIONAL PARK, JUST SOUTH OF GILLIES BAY

Nanoose Bay on Vancouver Island, and Hadley Lake on Lasqueti), *two* distinct freshwater forms evolved. One type preys on crustaceans and insect larvae along the bottom of the lake; the other catches tiny invertebrates in surface waters. The two varieties are able to interbreed but mostly don't.

We stop at Priest Lake, which is right beside the highway between Van Anda and Gillies Bay and is easy to approach. To us, the lake looks perfectly normal. On close inspection we see that its alkaline waters are dense with aquatic vegetation and insect life. Yellow pond-lilies bloom; on their floating leaves dozens of little brown frogs warm themselves in the sun's rays. At the edge of the lake we can clearly make out the five-centimetre-long sticklebacks. It's mating season, and the males sport bright red throats and iridescent blue eyes and flanks. They zigzag in front of the drabber, egg-swollen females, doing intricate dances. The fish we watch are streamlined and slender, and we presume that they must be the limnetic form, which feeds in open waters. The benthics, or bottom feeders, are larger and chunkier. These "species pairs," as scientists call them, show many other variations, too, including fewer, smaller spines and less heavily armoured lateral "plates" on the benthics, and different styles of gill rakers, internal comb-like structures used to sieve tiny food particles from the water. All of these features have developed over a few thousand years—a mere snap of the fingers in evolutionary terms.

No one knows exactly how such fishy transformations have occurred, or why they're proceeding so rapidly. One theory suggests that the lakes were invaded twice. The benthics, which are the more changed from their original shape, must have arrived first. Later, a second wave of sticklebacks turned up to find the best hunting grounds occupied but managed to adapt and survive anyway. A different theory holds that one single population split into two, taking advantage of separate feeding niches. If so, however, what is so unusual about these six lakes that this process happened nowhere else?

For evolutionary biologists, the opportunity to observe the rapid diversification of one species into several via natural selection (a process of speciation known as adaptive radiation) has astounding scientific value. Even better, researchers can compare parallel but separate instances of speciation taking place in one convenient area. In other words, the Paxton Lake stickleback pairs are not the same as the pairs in the Vananda Creek lakes, and the Enos Lake pairs are different still. And there are other unusual sticklebacks in BC lakes, especially in the Queen Charlotte Islands, where unarmoured and giant black forms of the fish are of special interest to researchers. Dr. Dolph Schluter, who is leading a stickleback team at the University of British Columbia, hopes that this tiny fish will help unravel some of evolution's fundamental mysteries over the next decade. BC's sticklebacks are on their way to becoming as famous as Darwin's finches.

One important question for scientists concerns how these fish should be classified. It's a bit of a taxonomist's nightmare. For instance, is each type, in each system of lakes, a separate species? DNA sampling is being done—plus plenty of arguing, one suspects. But this research is not mere technical hair-splitting; it can have profound effects on conservation efforts. Canada's new Species at Risk Act (SARA) requires that, after a complex and lengthy listing process, detailed recovery strategies be developed to protect each lifeform deemed sufficiently rare and imperilled. Four distinct sticklebacks—the limnetic and benthic forms from Paxton and the Vananda Creek lakes—are presently listed under SARA, while the two Enos Lake forms have been recognized as endangered and are expected to be officially listed soon.

A stickleback pairs recovery team, co-chaired by Jordan Rosenfeld of BC's Ministry of Water, Land and Air Protection and Dan Sneep of Fisheries and Oceans Canada, was formed in 2003. The process of crafting a strategy to protect these fish promises to be slow, however, as a consensus must be reached between federal and provincial scientists and bureaucrats, and with surrounding landowners and mineral leaseholders.

A SUMMER CAMP AT GILLIES BAY ON TEXADA ISLAND

A series of public meetings is scheduled for late 2004. What should be done in the meantime? Not much, according to the provincial government, which has approved logging plans in the Vananda Creek watershed. It's business as usual, apparently.

But these curious creatures, so important to science, clearly need some kind of immediate interim protection. Any number of dangers might wipe them out. They could be devastated by logging, road-construction, mining or the release of some toxin into their one and only home. Soil erosion, for instance, is already causing Enos Lake on Vancouver Island to become turbid, and the murk is interfering with the mating practices of the resident sticklebacks. The benthic and limnetic forms are unable to distinguish each other accurately and are hybridizing at a rapid rate. An even more dire scenario has already occurred in Lasqueti's Hadley Lake, where some idiot introduced a predatory bullhead in the early 1990s. In a stark example of the fragility of any localized wildlife population, both varieties of the Hadley stickleback are now extinct, eradicated from the face of the earth in less than one decade.

PORTLOCK POINT LIGHT GUARDS THE EASTERN CORNER OF PREVOST ISLAND.

Gulf Islands National Park Reserve

A cause for celebration

The natural world asserts itself as soon as Katherine and I leave our Prevost Island campsite and paddle round Peile Point. A bald eagle stoops beside us to grab a tiny fish dropped by a gull, transferring its catch from claw to beak with one deft move. Four skittish Angora goats, farmed on Prevost for their fleece, jump up from a mossy cliff where they're warming themselves in the morning sun and regard us with cautious disdain.

A surprising breeze from the northwest combines with an ebb tide to bowl us south along Trincomali Channel toward the Charles Rocks, where we can see movement. Seals? No, sea lions, a dozen or more. The huge animals lurch into the water and begin gliding toward us. We give them plenty of leeway and land nearby at tiny Hawkins Islet, which is covered with wildflowers and budding Garry oaks. The star-sapphire petals of common camas, waist high, form spectacular drifts; pink sea-blush blossoms are the size of golf balls.

These are just a few of the springtime delights of exploring BC's new Gulf Islands National Park Reserve, established in May 2003. Over the past ten years an array of properties—known collectively as the Pacific Marine Heritage Legacy—has been purchased for the park. Much of Prevost's north end was acquired for this purpose (in 1995, for about $2.2 million), as were chunks of North Pender, Saturna and Mayne, and the smaller islands of Georgeson, Tumbo and Russell. The area's existing provincial and regional parks have been folded into the new preserve, along with other Crown lands, including numerous miniature islets and reefs, such as Hawkins.

Knowing that the Gulf Islands are best visited in the off-season, before summer's surge of visitors, we make our initial investigation of the new park in early May, launching our kayaks at Saltspring Island's Ganges Harbour. A leisurely journey alongside the private Chain Islands, then a hop and a skip across the entrances to Welbury Bay and Long Harbour, brings us in less than an hour to Nose Point and an easy 800-metre crossing of Captain Passage to James Bay and Prevost Island.

About five kilometres long and two wide, Prevost was for many years the largest Gulf Island entirely in private hands—and is still the largest without ferry service. Riven by deep inlets and bays, it lies at the heart of the archipelago. Most of Prevost is farmland, stocked with free-ranging cattle, sheep and goats, and off-limits to visitors, who can still admire a shoreline dotted in spring with red-flowering currant, orange honeysuckle, broad-leaved stonecrop, strawberries and lichen-striped Rocky Mountain juniper.

The first settlers took up land in the late 1860s. A lighthouse was built at Portlock Point in 1896. In March 1964, shocked residents of Galiano, Mayne and North Pender islands heard an explosion and saw the station erupt in shooting flames. Ferries stopped and sent off shore parties. The Coast Guard arrived. Tragically, keeper James Heanski died in the blaze, which took hours to control. All the buildings were destroyed except for the tower, and the station was never rebuilt. Today the Portlock Point light is automated. When we step ashore there we find remnant daffodils blooming beside the old concrete foundations.

We push on to Prevost's south coast and the white shell beaches of the Red Islets, a good spot for lunch and for poking around tidepools alive with anemones, hermit crabs, chitons and limpets. In the afternoon, our twelve-kilometre circumnavigation of Prevost and its rocky satellites is easily concluded. One of these outliers, not part of the national park, is Secret Island, whose thirty-eight owners have really let the cat out of the bag, announcing their presence to the world with a clutter of cabins and docks. From there it's just a short jaunt back to James Bay and the only official campsite on Prevost so far, at an old orchard beside O'Reilly Beach.

The long narrow indentations on the west side of Prevost—Selby Cove, Annette Inlet, Glenthorne Passage—we leave for the next day's outing. Prevost's agricultural heritage is most visible on the isthmus between shallow Annette Inlet, lined with middens and mudflats, and Ellen Bay on the south end of the island. From our kayaks, we can see the workings of a substantial farm that dates back to 1924, when Digby Hussey (or DH) de Burgh, a descendant of Ireland's most powerful medieval clan, bought the island.

The de Burghs were French aristocrats; taming foreign lands was in their blood. After the Norman conquest of Britain, one de Burgh became Lord Governor of Ireland (the surnames Bourke and Burke derive from de Burgh); another was made Earl of Kent. Digby Hussey's Christian names, and those of his sons Hubert and Harlowen, who kept the Prevost farm going, can be traced back in history to the eleventh century. DH spent time on Saltspring in the 1890s but went home at the turn of the century to run the family estates. He returned, however, farmed on Prevost and went into business in Vancouver, where he died in 1951. The siren call of the Gulf Islands proved too strong for him, as it does for many visitors.

The Gulf Islands National Park Reserve will be a boon to ecotourism in the area, certainly, but that is not why it was formed. The park protects representative portions of some of Canada's rarest and most endangered ecosystems, particularly those of the Douglas-fir and Garry oak, which are under heavy pressure from development and urbanization. Indeed, less than 1 percent of the original coastal Douglas-fir forest that once covered this region is in its natural state today.

Rich, diverse marine ecosystems are also preserved by the park, with 200 metres of ocean adjacent to all park lands falling under federal protection and management. Although this may be the country's fifth smallest national park, with a total area of only thirty-three square kilometres (including a twenty-five-metre intertidal zone), it safeguards a priceless heritage.

Katherine and I decide that our next marine excursion into the park should be to South Pender, which is fairly remote by Gulf Islands standards but not nearly as isolated as Prevost. This is because North Pender has regular ferry service and receives a slew of summer tourists, many of whom visit South Pender by driving over the narrow bridge joining the two islands.

Last century, there was only one Pender Island. In 1903 the federal government went to the trouble to cut the narrow isthmus that linked the island's two main sections and blast out a navigable passage. In those days all travel was done by boat. The Canal, as it's known, eliminated an arduous detour for settlers and introduced a more convenient route for steamships. After it was completed, of course, islanders clamoured for a bridge to reconnect the severed parts. They clamoured for more than half a century, until 1956, when today's one-laner finally opened.

We find a temporary home at Beaumont, a fifty-eight-hectare former provincial marine park, which has been combined with an adjacent former regional park, Mount Norman, and made part of the new national park reserve. Visitor numbers are modest here, as there's no auto access to this lovely site on the north shore of Bedwell Harbour; you arrive by boat or else make a forty-minute hike in from Ainslie Point Road. Even so, most of the fifteen non-reservable tentsites, set in exquisite arbutus groves beside two fine shale beaches, are in use when we arrive in late July.

Bedwell Harbour is a delight, but it's hardly a wilderness experience for kayakers. Beaumont, for instance, looks out at a busy private marina and government wharf where US vessels clear customs on arrival in Canadian waters. There must be eighty boats, many of them gigantic floating palaces, anchored or docked in the bay while we're staying at the campsite.

But if you can't avoid 'em, join 'em, right? We decide to take advantage of the local amenities and are soon referring to our expedition as "pub kayaking." There's been many a time, huddled under a dripping tree somewhere on the central BC coast, that I've wished I were a fifteen-minute paddle from a spot like the Poets' Cove Pub, where you can enjoy tasty meals on an outdoor patio overlooking the sea. Later, we also drift into nearby Port Browning and have lunch at another pub-café combo with an excellent waterfront view. One evening, along with visiting family members, we head inland a few kilometres to the Inn at Pender Island, where Memories, an attractive restaurant, is located.

After this latter feast, we resolve to shake off any incipient "kayak potato" tendencies by paddling right round South Pender, a sixteen-kilometre trip that takes about four hours of actual travel time in fair weather. It's calm and sunny when we set off. All along the island's south and east coasts huge recreational homes alternate with rustic cottages from an earlier era. Belted kingfishers announce our approach with dry, rasping calls. Pretty pocket beaches, some with steps that lead to the network of narrow island roads, beckon whenever our efforts flag.

From Gowlland Point on the island's southwest side, we can gaze across Boundary Pass to the San Juan Islands in the US, only six kilometres away. One night, in fact, we're surprised to find ourselves sharing Beaumont park with a dozen kayakers from Portland, Oregon, who had paddled over that morning from Stuart Island just across the border.

We cross Canned Cod and Camp bays, and sneak between Blunden Islet and Teece Point at South Pender's western edge, then paddle along the relatively uninhabited north shore with its wonderful views across Plumper Sound to the steep,

SALT WATER KILLED THE TREES ON THIS CABBAGE ISLAND MARSH.

almost treeless bluffs of Saturna Island. Before we know it we've reached the Canal separating North and South Pender, and it's time to decide which pub to hit for lunch.

Not far away, North Pender has its own repertoire for paddlers, from the marshland bird sanctuary at Medicine Beach, where we first launched our kayaks, to Roesland and the Roe Lake/Malahat lands, purchased for the national park reserve. Fifteen-hectare Roesland was bought from the Davidson family in 1998 for $2.6 million; for decades it had been a well-known resort, with enviable beaches, woods and clearings. The 215-hectare Roe Lake property, with its uplands, second-growth forest and generous waterfront, cost $3.25 million and was acquired from a German syndicate.

The Canal, though entirely artificial, is a paddler's playground. It's only about twenty-five metres wide, though deep enough for most boats. When the current is right, kayakers can whip along its entire 150-metre length in mere minutes—from Shark Cove in the north, protected by the crooked gravel finger of Mortimer Spit, to Bedwell Harbour in the south.

On the western edge of the Canal, a shell beach has formed below one of the best middens I've ever seen. The eroded banks above the beach are a window into history and a place of wonder for archaeologists (though it's against the law for unauthorized persons to disturb middens or remove any material from them), who have found many bone and stone artifacts among the thick layers of clam shell. These ancient refuse pits were created 2,000 to 6,000 years ago while Saanich and Songhees First Nations groups camped here in the summers.

As we prepare to leave, Katherine hoots at me and points to the water ahead of her kayak. Three furry, whiskered noses can be seen moving rapidly toward shore. A moment later, three glistening river otters jump out onto some flat rocks and stand motionless, watching us intently from a distance of about five metres. Two juveniles soon join them, and finally two more adults, and the entire family cavorts while we struggle to stay in position against the current. Finally, we head back toward Beaumont, encountering more healthy-looking, well-fed otters on the way. One curious kit almost jumps into my cockpit while it practises dives near a sheltered dock.

For our third foray into the national park reserve, we hook up with paddling partners Elaine and Mike, who figure in several of these stories. Our goal is to paddle to the easternmost point of the Gulf Islands archipelago, where the waters of Georgia Strait accelerate as they swerve and squeeze through Boundary

Pass. We put in from Mayne Island, at Bennett Bay, and beat our way south against the tide, along Samuel and Saturna islands. On a chain of islets to the east we can see—and hear—groups of Steller's sea lions lolling and arguing in the sun. It's June, our first serious outing of the season; a year has passed since visiting Prevost and South Pender, and I, for one, am feeling another year older.

A pair of islands, Cabbage and Tumbo, lie off Saturna's southeast shores. We aim at Cabbage, only 4.5 hectares in size, a former provincial marine park and, we've heard, a gem of a place. Tumbo, much larger at 121 hectares, was purchased in 1997 for $3.7 million from its Californian owner through the Pacific Marine Heritage Legacy. Both are now part of the new national park, along with several other substantial properties on Saturna itself: around Narvaez Bay and Mount Warburton Pike, at Winter Cove and along the southern coastline from Bruce to Trueworthy bights (including the ruins of an old farm and sandstone quarry at Taylor Point). Almost two-thirds of the island is protected.

Cabbage, fringed with sand and shaded by groves of arbutus, turns out to be an excellent spot to pitch a tent. Gnarled Rocky Mountain junipers arch over pathways that burrow through the salal. A strange little marsh, dotted with the spindly grey trunks of trees killed when salt water inundated them in a 1982 winter storm, frames a view of Mount Baker. Beside the marsh, a bald eagle guards its eaglet-laden nest high in a sentinel Douglas-fir. We camp on the island for three days and check out the neighbourhood.

Cabbage is wonderful, but Tumbo, next door, is a masterpiece—an unspoiled example of what all the Gulf Islands might have looked like a century and a half ago. It takes its name from the tombolos, or sand spits, that extend from its extremities.

ERODED SANDSTONE AT THE EASTERN TIP OF TUMBO ISLAND

You can't camp there, but you can walk a network of trails that runs the island's entire length. Behind a lovely pebble beach at the south end of Tumbo, where giant Garry oaks and arbutus flourish, a broad cattail marsh supports a mob of red-winged blackbirds. A log-cabin homestead, which may date to the 1880s, sits beneath tall poplar trees beside a field of golden, waving grass. A coal mine on the island was worked by resident Japanese miners in the early 1900s.

One day we round Tumbo Point in our kayaks and begin to cross Tumbo Channel to East Point on Saturna Island, where an old lighthouse stands. The tide is ebbing, and after about ten minutes I notice with surprise that, beyond East Point, Vancouver Island seems to be moving south at a rapid rate. Behind me Tumbo is already a kilometre away and receding fast. We are being swept into Boundary Pass, where giant freighters ply, and out toward the San Juan Islands.

We alter course to improve our chances of reaching Saturna, but it soon becomes clear that we will overshoot it. Even worse, we realize with mounting alarm that we're being drawn toward aptly named Boiling Reef, a ragged chunk of rock off the tip of East Point. It had looked passive enough from a distance, but as we get closer we see that the current is creating a vicious set of standing waves at the reef's edge. In fact, all the waters in the vicinity seem to be converging on this wave train, bearing us with them.

Fear enters the picture. We start paddling back the way we've come, away from the rip and directly against the current. We have to work hard to make even the faintest progress. Katherine is growing exhausted, and I know she'll be unable to keep up this pace for long.

A sailboat behind us, motoring north from the US toward Vancouver, comes closer and closer and, finally, I flag it down. The skipper throws us a line. Mike and Elaine, in a faster double kayak and now free of the necessity of waiting for us, paddle on at full speed and make better way against the current. Katherine and I, in our singles, hang on for dear life as we fishtail through the ocean behind the sailboat. We wrap the rope around our backs, steer with our rudders and hope that a sudden side wave or lurch of the boat won't capsize us. After what seems like a decade we pass our labouring comrades and draw near to shore, where the current falters and we can cast adrift from our host. After a rest and some lunch, we paddle back to camp along the carved sandstone bluffs that line Tumbo Channel. Thank you, thank you, skipper and crew of the *Marta II*—whoever you are. May you never again have to rescue paddlers from the whirlpools of Boiling Reef.

What would have happened if we'd managed to skirt the tide rip and been sucked out into Boundary Pass? Nothing much, hopefully. The wind was light, the weather warm; we had food and water. Eventually, the tide in the pass would have turned and driven us back toward land. I think we'd have survived. But we would have been wiped out from our exertions and might have spent many hours at sea. And we could easily have ended up far from campsite and gear.

Tumbo Channel, we later learn, is unusual in that the tide there never truly turns. The current always flows southward. Boiling Reef is a graveyard for several vessels. It was after a ship went aground there in 1886, in fact, that land was purchased for the East Point lighthouse.

After returning to Bennett Bay from Cabbage Island, we decide we need a night on Mayne to recover from all the excitement. We stay at Seal Beach, an idyllic private campground with an outdoor shower and hot tub, perfect for kayakers, then dine at Springwater Lodge beside Miners Bay. Next morning we take a ferry to Swartz Bay on Vancouver Island, drive to Sidney, launch at Roberts Bay and kayak out through a tiny archipelago known as the Little Group, riding the strong currents of Haro Strait south toward Sidney Island. We look forward to continuing our recuperation for a few days at Sidney Spit, one of the finest campsites in the region.

There's lots to see, I figure, in this southerly annex to the Gulf Islands National Park Reserve. Two other portions of the new park—D'Arcy Island, which served as a leper colony from 1891 to 1924, and Isle-de-Lis, both former provincial marine parks—are an easy commute from Sidney Spit. There's a seabird sanctuary and ecological reserve at Mandarte Island, which must be admired from a respectful distance. And there are dozens of fascinating private islands to paddle around, including 315-hectare James, once home to a large explosives factory and its worker village. James Island, owned by Seattle's McCaw family, was on the market recently for a mere $50 million US. Mind you, it does come with a Jack Nicklaus-designed golf course, six upscale cottages, docks, airstrip, maintenance centre and ten kilometres of gorgeous beach.

Sidney Island has beaches in abundance, too, visible as we sweep into the vast lagoon that dominates its northern end. This is where the 140-hectare park is located, and it's a popular spot for boaters on hot weekends. Sidney Spit's thirty-five-site campground usually has plenty of space in the off-season and on weekdays. A small, passenger-only private ferry operates from Sidney during the summer, but its schedule can be erratic and should be confirmed in advance.

So pleasant is Sidney Spit—and so unfavourable are the tides and currents at the time of our visit—that we decide to postpone a trip to the surrounding islands and opt instead for hiking and birdwatching. The big lagoon is one of the richest bird habitats in the region, especially for great blue herons. Two long, constantly shifting sand arms embrace its muddy shallows, and it's a good stroll, six kilometres or more, from the tip of Sidney Spit to Hook Point at the end of the more southerly arm.

At least thirty herons are feeding while we're there, along with many gulls, cormorants and other birds. One of BC's largest heron breeding colonies (over one hundred nests in 1987) once existed beside the lagoon. The Canadian Wildlife Service built a cabin there, and research scientist Robert Butler gathered data and later wrote a book on the species and its conservation requirements. The herons abandoned their colony in the early 1990s, probably because of predation by the area's many bald eagles. We also see nighthawks, dozens of white-crowned sparrows and an osprey pair.

Sidney and James are quite different from other Gulf Islands. For one thing, they are glacial moraines—glorified sand and gravel bars that are rapidly eroding and changing shape. The fine sediments of the lagoon, which shelter the marine creatures that herons and other birds feed on, were once an attraction for industry, too. The Sidney Island Brick & Tile Company, located where the campground is today, operated in the years before World War I, supplying its products to the Empress Hotel. You can still see old foundations; broken bricks line the adjacent shoreline.

The island was known as Sallas to the Coast Salish people. It was the site of an 1860 Hudson's Bay Company land auction, but the opening bid of six shillings an acre (about forty dollars in Canadian funds today) was too much for most attendees. Sidney changed hands many times. By 1910 pheasants and peafowl had been introduced for the hunting pleasure of Victoria businessmen. James Island, also an early hunting preserve, was stocked with European fallow deer. These small spotted animals swam over to Sidney and proliferated; now they roam the island in voracious, easily visible herds, eating every green thing they encounter.

We follow the deer east and come to a fence and signs informing us that the rest of the island is privately owned by the Sallas Forest Limited Partnership. Since 1980 this group of investors has built family cabins and practised selective

KATHERINE WAITS FOR A VESSEL TO PASS THROUGH THE NARROW CANAL BETWEEN NORTH AND SOUTH PENDER ISLANDS.

logging. Recently, however, Islands Trust approved a development plan for Sidney Island, and Sallas has begun selling its holdings as eagerly as the Hudson's Bay did 145 years ago.

The real-estate operation is an unusual one; twenty-four strata-titled portions have been carved out of the Sallas-owned part of the island, each one containing several individual building lots. Roads, trails, a dock, an airstrip and 600 hectares of forest will be owned in common. Sensitive zones, including ponds, fragile bluffs and a large area at the east end of Sidney, have been protected with restrictive covenants. Every building lot has waterfront or water views—and water to drink, as well. It's a nice deal if you have a spare $200,000 or so lying about. The price works out to be somewhat more than six shillings an acre, but it's still a bargain compared to James Island next door.

ROUNDING THE EASTERN CORNER OF SOUTH PENDER ISLAND
WITH SATURNA IN THE BACKGROUND

Eventually, the time arrives for us to paddle home. After we pack up and truck our gear down to the water's edge, Mike bends over his double kayak to grab the carrying handle and we hear a gasp of pain. He doesn't straighten up. He can't, in fact. He's thrown his back out so badly he can scarcely walk, let alone kayak. Several hours of stretching and massage don't help a bit. What to do? There's no way Elaine can paddle the double by herself, even if Mike could get into the kayak, which he can't.

Fortunately, the little ferry is running. The skipper doesn't like to take kayaks, but we talk him into relaxing the rules. Mike watches in chagrin as the rest of us haul and lift and strap our bags and boats to the ferry's cabin roof. Back in Sidney we treat him to a burger and a beer. Fortunately, after a week of physical therapy, he recovers. We're grateful that

Mike's back didn't seize in the middle of Tumbo Channel. And we celebrate the range of experiences one can sample in the Gulf Islands National Park Reserve: bliss on Hawkins Islet, terror at Boiling Reef, creature comforts on South Pender, rides home from Sidney Spit. BC's newest national park will help preserve the wealth of nature, to be sure, but also a unique way of life for its fortunate human residents.

LEKWILTOK FIRST NATION POLES OUTSIDE THE KWAGIULTH MUSEUM
AT CAPE MUDGE VILLAGE ON QUADRA ISLAND

Discovery Islands Lodge

Exploring Quadra and Read

From the third-floor lounge of Discovery Islands Lodge, we can see Read and Maurelle islands to the east across Hoskyn Channel. Whiterock Passage between the two is a vanishing point in the distance, and each receding ridgeline is a different shade of blue. To the north, Antonio Point, Surge Narrows Provincial Marine Park and the islands of the Settlers Group form a playground for paddlers unfazed by active tidal waters. On a calm day, in fact, you can hear the roar of the rapids in Beazley Passage. A range of snow-capped mainland peaks, lorded over by Hat Mountain and Dudley Cone, backdrops the scene. In the entire panorama we glimpse two boats and exactly four distant buildings. The rest is forest, sea and sky.

Katherine and I are here on the remote east coast of Quadra Island, 185 kilometres northwest of Vancouver, to try out an unfamiliar style of accommodation. On this afternoon in late

May we're lucky enough to be the lodge's only guests. Our belongings are spread generously throughout the lounge or common room—the heart of the resort with its well-equipped kitchen, comfortable sofas, balcony and enormous, polished wooden table and benches.

Discovery Islands Lodge is the brainchild of Ralph and Lannie Keller. It's a recent example of a new and heartening trend in BC tourism: stylish yet affordable resorts with private rooms and shared facilities that are geared to the self-propelled crowd. The vision, says Ralph, is to provide an alternative to the fully catered touring that he and Lannie have offered for so long. Here independent travellers can use the lodge as a base while exploring the Discovery Islands, which are full of interest to kayakers. "It's dedicated," he says, "to those who want to rent or bring their own boats and explore the area on their own."

Ralph and Lannie, proprietors of Coast Mountain Expeditions, are a story in themselves. From Coast Mountain Lodge, their main facility on Read Island, they have been leading kayaking tours and getaways for seventeen years. Ralph hails from Lantzville on Vancouver Island, Lannie from St. Louis. They moved to Read, an island without ferry service, over two decades ago as young, naive homesteaders. After raising two children, Emily and Albert, there, they gradually became "politicised," as Ralph, research and policy chair for the Green Party of BC, puts it, when resource industries began closing in on their coastal paradise.

One day Katherine and I paddle from the hostel to the west side of Read Island and the tiny village of Surge Narrows, a cluster of homes and floats with a general store, post office and a delightful twelve-student elementary school. Then we hike for an hour and a quarter over peaceful back roads to Coast Mountain's headquarters, spread out beside Evans Bay,

RETURNING HOME TO DISCOVERY ISLANDS LODGE AFTER A DAY OF KAYAKING

where staff are sprucing up the cabins, creekside sauna, grounds and dock for the coming season. In the rustic cedar lodge, a nineteenth-century Steinway piano, an heirloom from Lannie's side of the family, dominates the common area. We meet Emily Keller in the huge garden, back home after a year's globe-trotting, where she'll work for the summer before returning to university. She kindly answers our questions about what it was like to grow up here. "Wonderful," she confirms. "That school had thirty students when I went to it. There were five other girls my age." Despite the heavy logging on Read, the Kellers' operation, with its composting outhouses, solar panels and micro-hydroelectric system, still has a modern-day touch of Swiss Family Robinson about it.

After hiking and paddling back to Discovery Islands Lodge, we shift next day from saltwater to freshwater and sample

Quadra's Main Lake Provincial Park. Only minutes by car from the hostel, the park encompasses three large, interconnected lakes—Main, Mine and Village Bay—where boaters and paddlers can stop at seven wilderness campsites. Village Bay, the southernmost lake, is home to many summer cabins and was once the site of a floating logging camp. The loggers dammed the exit to the lake and, when water levels were high, floated logs down a short stream to Village Bay on Hoskyn Channel. This practice, however, prevented salmon from spawning and was unappreciated by the local Lekwiltok people, who once lived on Village Bay in a community named Yakwen. To protect their fish stocks they blew the dam up in the dead of night.

Mine and Main lakes, north of Village Bay Lake and joined by narrow but current-free channels, are quite pristine. Lake kayaking is a peaceful alternative to the ocean, and the campsites, most with small sand beaches, are idyllic. From the northeast corner of island-studded Main Lake I hike a 1.6-kilometre trail to Yeatman Bay on Okisollo Channel and back, disturbing a barred owl en route, which flaps on massive wings up from the ground to a nearby branch. For once I have binoculars with me, and we regard each other with intense interest for a full fifteen minutes.

Back at the hostel we examine our quarters more closely. The red-brown structure, along with its wharf, was originally part of an aquaculture operation, an unsuccessful early-1980s joint venture between the BC government and a Norwegian company. Ralph Keller takes great glee in having acquired a building once devoted to the environmentally unsound business of fish farming and turning it to more eco-friendly purposes. The Douglas-fir floors have been refinished and the inner walls resurfaced with native pine. Seven simple rooms are equipped with bunks and a few double beds so that singles, couples and families—up to eighteen people, if necessary—can stay. New kayak-friendly floating docks have been attached to the wharf. The kitchen, where guests cook for themselves, has a heavy-duty propane range and just about everything one could possibly need for preparing meals and storing food.

While Discovery Islands Lodge has really been designed with kayakers in mind, it's equally well suited to bikers or hikers, or to those who simply want to explore the sights of Quadra. One day, for instance, we set off to investigate the island's northern backwoods. First we take a side road to the former Hoskyn Channel steamship landing of Bold Point, which once had a store and post office, a hotel and a cattle ranch. Now there are just a handful of rural homes and a seriously decaying wharf.

The northernmost point you can reach by road on Quadra is Granite Bay, a small inlet off much larger Kanish Bay. From about 1890 to 1925, one of the region's largest railway logging camps was located here. A few people still live in the area; several elderly live-aboard boats and floating homes are anchored offshore. These waters, we note, would make another good kayaking destination; there are all kinds of islands in Kanish Bay, while an adjacent body of water, Small Inlet, is protected by a provincial marine park. From Small Inlet, a short portage trail leads to Waiatt Bay on the east side of Quadra and nearby Octopus Islands Provincial Marine Park. Another trail leads to Newton Lake.

We promise ourselves a decent hike in the afternoon, and have any number of choices thanks to the efforts of the Quadra Trails Committee, which publishes a hiking guide and has developed a wonderful, well-posted route system for island

SCENES FROM READ ISLAND: THE SAUNA AT COAST MOUNTAIN LODGE *(above)*
AND THE TINY COMMUNITY OF SURGE NARROWS *(below)*

rambling. Who can resist a name like the Chinese Mountains Trail? We start through an understorey of delicate willows, bald-hip rose, ocean spray and huckleberry, and past giant bigleaf maples. Fresh young bracken ferns line the path. Soon we're climbing in and out of second-growth forest and along mossy bluffs. Eventually, at the summit we're rewarded with huge views of all the Discovery Islands, the mountains of Vancouver Island and the BC mainland, and south down the Strait of Georgia. It's a grand finale to an excellent day.

Visitors should really also spend at least a day on the south part of Quadra, where most of the island's 3,500 residents live. We drive to Cape Mudge, a Lekwiltok First Nation community just south of Quathiaski Cove, where the ferry crosses to Campbell River, and we stop for brunch at the Lovin' Oven. Our goal is to visit the Kwagiulth Museum and its potlatch regalia, confiscated by the feds in the 1920s when potlatching was illegal and only returned in 1979. But the museum is closed. We admire carved poles and the 1931 church, now non-denominational, with its stained-glass window of a fishing boat at sea. The village, perched on the edge of Discovery Passage, is a lovely peaceful setting.

Cape Mudge lighthouse began operations in 1898, warning vessels away from the cape's dangerous reefs and surging tidal waters. Despite a heavy shower, we trudge from the station along the shore to Tsa-Kwa-Luten Lodge, a spectacular hotel owned by Quadra's Lekwiltok community. Just beyond the lodge are grassy bluffs atop crumbling sand cliffs. This wonderful location, with its long views down the Strait of Georgia, was the site of one of the few First Nations villages that Captain Vancouver actually visited. Both Vancouver and his naturalist, Archibald Menzies, left detailed accounts of their excursion here in 1792.

The most beautiful part of Quadra, for most people, is the long, narrow neck of Rebecca Spit, set aside in 1958 as one of BC's first marine parks. Trails wind through old groves of Douglas-fir along the shores of Drew Harbour, a protected anchorage formed by the spit and much favoured by boaters. All kinds of ducks and seabirds feed here; we saw surf scoters, buffleheads, harlequins, mergansers, common goldeneyes and loons. The Quadra community holds May Day celebrations at Rebecca Spit, keeping alive a tradition that has lasted now for more than one hundred years.

Adjacent to Drew Harbour is Heriot Bay, where the Heriot Bay Inn is worth a visit whether you stay over or not. The L-shaped structure, built in 1916 to replace an 1894 loggers' watering hole, is one of the few heritage coastal hotels still operating in BC. The rooms are basic but perfectly adequate, and have full bathrooms but no TV. There's a friendly year-round pub at one end of the building and a summer-only restaurant at the other. This part of Quadra is well within reach of paddlers staying at Discovery Islands Lodge.

In July and August, when the lodge is in full swing, the Kellers will add breakfast, kayak rentals and day tours to the hostel experience. The tours will lead beginners and experienced paddlers into Surge Narrows Park, with its exciting back eddies and swirling waters, and take them to intimate vantage points where participants can get out and absorb the full impact of the tidal rapids as they build to nine-knot velocities. "At first," says Ralph, "we thought the rapids might be a liability for the lodge, but now we see that they can become a real attraction."

For us, Discovery Island Lodge's attractions are numerous, both for day trips and as a source of creature comforts at the beginning and end of multi-day excursions to kayaking havens like the Octopus and Rendezvous islands, only a day's paddle away. With similar hostel-style kayak retreats springing up in Barkley Sound and the Johnstone Strait area, the resort could become a starting point in what I've always thought should be the ultimate ecotourism goal for this province: lodge-to-lodge paddling along much of BC's fabulous coastline.

WITH FRIENDS AT SOUTH THORMANBY ISLAND

The Thormanbies

Island siblings a study in opposites

Good beaches are hard to come by after you leave Vancouver and head northwest up the Strait of Georgia. Oh, there are a few sandy pockets, certainly, hidden here and there along the coast, but you must travel seventy kilometres before finding anything that rivals, say, Vancouver's Spanish Banks or Jericho or Wreck Beach. Even then, the silvery strands I'm thinking of are easy to miss, as they're mostly hidden away in a secluded north-facing basin and somewhat screened from passing boat traffic.

These are the beaches of the Thormanby Islands, and they form about as pleasant a destination as one can wish to reach in southwestern BC. The islands are separated from the Sunshine Coast by one-kilometre-wide Welcome Pass. There's a government wharf at Vaucroft on North Thormanby Island, though the beach there is inferior in quality to Gill Beach on

South Thormanby, which is composed of the finest white sand. Grassy Point, where the two islands are temporarily linked at low tide and where Buccaneer Bay Provincial Marine Park is located, is also a big triangular beach.

This one-hectare recreational hotspot can get jammed in July and August, but it is idyllic in the off-season and on most summer weekdays. Another nearby marine park, 461-hectare Simson, which covers much of South Thormanby, is virtually unvisited. Simson doesn't have the sandy beaches, but it's a gem nonetheless. Both islands are intriguing from just about any perspective you care to imagine. They have neat histories, weird geologies and great natural beauty. I'm lucky enough to live in the neighbourhood, and I visit them as often as possible, usually by kayak.

From the water you can see how the islands differ. North Thormanby is a glacial moraine, a light-coloured pile of silt, gravel and stones that has been heaped and layered by the giant ice sheets that once trundled up and down Georgia Strait. As islands go, North Thormanby is a youngster—only a few tens of thousands of years old. Its crumbling cliffs, which are almost identical to those of Point Grey in Vancouver, continue to provide material for the gently sloping beaches, which pretty well circle the island. Large boulders, deposited helter-skelter by the retreating glaciers in the collar of shallow water that surrounds the island, provide an occasional surprise for unitiated boaters.

In many spots you can easily make out the different glacial striations. The oldest deposits—deep swaths of sand and gravel known as the Cowichan Head and Semiahmoo drifts—are below sea level and out of sight, left there 40,000 to 50,000 years ago. The next layer, and the most visible one, consists of fine silt laid down 25,000 to 29,000 years ago;

these horizontal beds of sediment, up to a hundred metres deep, are the Quadra sands, and they form most of North Thormanby, Savary, Hernando, Marina, Harwood, Kuper, Denman, James and Sidney islands, plus Point Grey, the east coast of Vancouver Island and parts of Quadra and Cortes islands. Then comes the Vashon till, dating back 14,000 to 18,000 years, a fairly thin band of gravel and rocks that represents the disappearing glaciers' parting gift. The top layer, wind-blown sand, is less than 10,000 years old. Fortunately for island residents, small pockets of potable ground water are trapped at various levels by narrow bands of clay.

South Thormanby, by comparison, is dark and hard. It is composed of fractured basalt, an igneous rock laid down tens of millions of years ago during a volcanic upheaval. Its jagged shoreline, indented by dozens of little coves, plunges straight into the ocean. Offshore islets and rocks shelter colonies of seals and sea lions but represent a menace to mariners. One hazard, Fraser Rock, proved so dangerous to navigation that it had to be blown apart—but not before claiming two well-known tugs, the *Commodore Straits* and the *Lornet*, and a barge fashioned from the hull of the *Princess Victoria*, one of the coast's most venerable steamships.

Where North Thormanby pushes up against the southern island, a narrow isthmus has formed, as has delightful, sandy Buccaneer Bay. Beside this body of water is the region's best real estate. A Sechelt First Nation village, no trace of which now remains, was likely located on this bay as well. The Sechelt people knew the Thormanby islands as Skoulap or Skwah-lahwt (there are numerous spelling variations). They reportedly maintained a fort there on the west coast and a lookout post on Spy Glass Hill, the islands' high point at 155 metres, to give early warning of raiders.

Above: THE BEACH AT GRASSY POINT IN BUCCANEER BAY

Below: A GIGANTIC BEAVER POND ENGULFS SOUTH THORMANBY'S FORMER FARM.

The Thormanby Islands owe their name to the horse that won the 1860 Derby at the famed English racetrack of Epsom Downs in Surrey. The crew of the *Plumper*, a naval survey ship working in the area at the time, must have been a betting crowd; they became so excited after hearing the news that they labelled everything in sight after the kingly sport. Buccaneer, for instance, was also a well-known horse from the era. Epsom, Derby and Oaks points all result from this naming binge (the Oaks was another major Epsom race), as do the Surrey Islands in Buccaneer Bay and Tattenham Ledge, which extends north from the tip of South Thormanby and was dubbed after a notorious corner on the Epsom course.

Between 1890 and 1892, a noted early Vancouver resident pre-empted most of South Thormanby. Calvert Simson had worked as storekeeper and postmaster at Gastown's historic Hastings Mill Store (now located in Pioneer Park at the foot of Alma Street and believed to be Vancouver's oldest structure). In 1891, finding himself between jobs, Simson built a simple cabin on the island and lived there for a year. If he had to get to Vancouver, he either rowed or else had his rowboat towed behind some obliging larger vessel.

After his rural sojourn Simson returned to the growing city and worked as a ship chandler, selling marine supplies at Dunn's and other companies, before he and Tom Balkwill went into business together and formed their own chandlery, Simson Balkwill, in 1908. During this period he could reach his country home by Union Steamship vessel, usually the *Comox*. He allowed numerous friends and business acquaintances to camp or put up simple summer abodes on Buccaneer Bay, charging them five dollars a year.

Around 1912 Simson cleared land on the island and erected a house and barn. He installed tenants, who operated a farm there until 1948. The Simson family also logged the property of its best timber. The farm buildings were not demolished until the late 1960s; you can still see their foundations. Since then, beavers have built a dam across the old drainage outlet from the farm meadows, and today the fields lie beneath a swampy five-hectare lake. Many waterfowl and other birds, including great blue herons and kingfishers, have been attracted to the site.

Simson and Balkwill turned out to be prescient businessmen, selling their chandlery, for cash, only six months before the great stock-market crash of October 1929. Calvert Simson died in 1959, aged ninety-seven, and left the island to his sons George and William (more commonly—and confusingly—known as Joe and Bob). George Simson, in an interview, said that Calvert had always regarded Thormanby as "an escape from the confinement of years of storekeeping for the freedom and solitude of wilderness living."

After Calvert's sons died, the family estate donated the eastern two-thirds of South Thormanby to the province for a park in 1982. The western third of the island, with its exquisite beaches, remained in the hands of the next generation of Simsons. A motley collection of about fifty summer cottages has grown up behind Gill Beach over a century and more, and this unusual private community, which operates as a kind of co-operative and has a similar atmosphere to Savary Island farther north, comes to life each summer, echoing with the calls of happy children. South Thormanby cottage lots and shares are mostly passed down within families and rarely come onto the market; newcomers must be approved by the other property owners.

North Thormanby is still in private hands. Most of the island is divided into two-hectare lots, some of which sport luxurious

ONE OF THE OLD COTTAGES ON BUCCANEER BAY'S GILL BEACH

recreational homes. A second quaint old resort community is located behind Vaucroft Beach. The BC Telephone Company maintained a hotel and summer camp there for its staff in the 1920s, and a cluster of cabins sprang up. A post office even operated for two summers. Steamships called at the Vaucroft dock with throngs of holiday-makers and also deposited people destined for Gill Beach on a float further down Buccaneer Bay.

Today, in summer, the bay is equally busy. And Simson Provincial Marine Park, with its alder-infested logging tracks and rocky viewpoints, is as quiet as ever. A large population of blacktail deer ghost through the second-growth forests of Douglas-fir and hemlock. Overgrown apple and cherry trees linger where the farmhouse once stood. Bald eagles and osprey circle overhead. You're only two hours from Vancouver on the Thormanby Islands, but they seem a world away.

AGATE BEACH NEAR TOW HILL IN NAIKOON PROVINCIAL PARK, GRAHAM ISLAND

Graham Island

Out of the shadow of glamorous Moresby

At the edge of the fine pebble beach, six great poles stare out at Hecate Strait with eloquent silence. Two painted cedar canoes, equally massive, ride at anchor in the bay. Days before our arrival, 5,000 guests had celebrated here during a week-long pole-raising festival. Every motel room and campsite on southern Graham Island was taken, the ferry booked solid for months beforehand. Now things have returned to normal and Qay'llnagaay is still.

A gang of crows patrols the shoreline in the spitting rain. Vehicles trickle into the parking lot. Located between the ferry terminus at Skidegate Landing and the large Haida village of Skidegate, Qay'llnagaay is the first stop most visitors make after arriving in the Queen Charlotte Islands. Here, along with the poles and the canoe shed, they find the small

Haida Gwaii Museum, one of the best in the province with a superb collection of photographs, carvings and other artifacts.

In the distant past, Qay'llnagaay was the site of Sea-Lion-Town, a famous "story" town associated with Haida origin myths. Now a $20-million, 6,300-square-metre cultural complex is rising on this spot, which will incorporate the museum, an arts centre (to be named after Bill Reid), canoe house, restaurant and hotel. Modelled on Haida architectural designs, the buildings will face the bay and resemble a traditional village. Most of the new poles, which represent southern Haida clans from Tanu, Ninstints, Cumshewa, Skedans, Skidegate and Chaatl, will become part of the structures. Eight more poles will be commissioned, many of them free-standing.

Qay'llnagaay makes a good starting and finishing point for a tour of 6,436-square-kilometre Graham Island, which is our mission this summer. Moresby Island to the south, with its Gwaii Haanas National Park Reserve and famed Haida village sites, seems to get all the press, but Graham, BC's largest island after Vancouver Island, is also an impressive place to visit. After seeing the museum and examining the new poles at leisure we drive to Queen Charlotte City, just down the road from the ferry landing. The tiny "city," strung out along the shore of Bearskin Bay, is really a village, picturesque and laid-back, with plenty of restaurants and hotels. I head straight to one of my favourite places: Northwest Coast Books, with its unparalleled First Nations section—the best in BC.

Bill Ellis established the bookstore as a little retirement project in the early 1980s, when he was in his sixties. It was fun to go in and browse through his stock, with its wonderful selection of out-of-print titles, and chat with Ellis, who was friendly and outgoing and unusually knowledgeable. He had become a specialist in Northwest Coast books, supplying rare

DON'T GET STUCK! A VEHICLE DRIVES DOWN NORTH BEACH, WHICH STRETCHES FOR FORTY KILOMETRES.

volumes to collectors and libraries from his Haida Gwaii outpost. After Ellis died in 2002, long-time employee Janet Brown became owner of the bookstore; Bill's son, David Ellis, who lives in Vancouver, is involved with the out-of-print inventory. On this occasion I come away with two modern classics: Robert Bringhurst's celebration of Haida mythtelling, *A Story as Sharp as a Knife*, and George MacDonald's masterful *Haida Monumental Art*.

Next day we drive back to Skidegate Landing, where I want to check out the original site of the Oil Works, an early island factory. Just before we get there a commotion in the ocean prompts us to stop and climb out on the rocks beside the inlet. Two gray whales are feeding close to shore, making tight circles as they dive again and again, stirring up the shallow water's muddy bottom. We're able to get directly above the animals, not ten metres away, and look straight down on their broad, barnacle-encrusted backs. We watch them in awe for almost half an hour.

Just west of the ferry terminal is a small beach overhung with foliage, where the remnant tracks of a rusty boat launch point into the clear waters of Sterling Bay. Belted kingfishers perch on old pilings. Behind the beach the land is choked with Nootka rose bushes, cow parsnip and thimbleberry. The big trees growing here—cottonwood, horse chestnut, oak, sequoia—are unusual ones for the region and were planted well over a century ago by the owners of the Oil Works. The oil in question was not petroleum but a rank substance produced by refining dogfish livers. The history of the site offers a small but intriguing look at the past.

West coast anglers normally disdain the spiny dogfish, also known as the grayfish or spurdog. This small common shark grows to about 1.5 metres and nine kilograms. It's a notorious hook-grabber when you're after more attractive prey. Ironically, the flesh of the dogfish is quite tasty when properly prepared; its skin makes a fine abrasive and the large liver is rich in vitamins. But there's something unnerving about the fierce, glassy-eyed predator. The commercial fishery for *Squalus acanthias* never amounted to much.

In the nineteenth century, though, dogfish oil was vital to local industry. It was a tanning agent, a lamp fuel and a lubricant for machinery of all kinds. The oil's most important use was to grease the skid roads that slid timber to Pacific Northwest sawmills. The skidgreaser, usually a young fellow on his first job, was covered in oil by the end of the day and smelled so foul that he was frequently forced to bunk in a separate building.

Dogfish were abundant and unexploited in Haida Gwaii in 1876, when William Sterling and his partners set up the Skidegate Oil Company. The enterprise depended on the labour of the Haida, who could catch up to 400 fish per man per day using herring-baited lines, each with hundreds of hooks. The ten or so white employees cooked the livers in large steam-heated tanks, skimmed off the oil, refined it in retorts and then filtered it through charcoal.

By the 1880s, the operation produced 160,000 litres of oil a year. It was mostly shipped south of the border, but also exported as far afield as Hawaii and China. Surveyor and author Newton Chittenden visited the works in 1884 and found them "a scene of great interest ... the shore covered with canvas, Indian men, women and children, dried halibut, herring spawn, fishing tackle, bedding and camp equipage." The oilery changed hands several times before closing in 1918. By then, the small community of Skidegate Landing had grown up around it.

An important part of the business was the company store, stocked with trade goods from Victoria and designed to recapture any monies earned by the Haida. At first the fishermen were paid in cash. Later, however, they were issued with cardboard scrip—now very rare and prized by collectors—printed in fifty-cent and one-dollar denominations. The scrip could only be exchanged for goods at the oilery store. It supposedly reduced opportunities for rash investments in illegal liquor.

I became interested in the Oil Works years ago after buying an old letter from the oilery, dated June 30, 1877, that described the venture and requested "a bottle of brandy" for "the boys."

Research at BC Archives in Victoria uncovered some of William Sterling's personal papers. They revealed that the real function of the scrip had been to prevent Haida fishermen from patronizing the Hudson's Bay store at Fort Simpson across Hecate Strait, where a wider range of goods was available at better prices.

Besides working at Sterling's oilery, the Haida also produced their own dogfish oil for sale to white traders. But the importance of the dogfish went well beyond the value of its oil. This animal, often in the form of the powerful shaman Qqaaxhadajaat, or Dogfish Woman, played a vital role in Haida myth and art. Qqaaxhadajaat was captured by dogfish and lived in their world, much to the sorrow of her husband, who searched for her for years. Robert Bringhurst, in *A Story as Sharp as a Knife*, suggests that her legend reflects "the permanence of love in a world filled with death and sudden disappearances." Sadly, most of the stories associated with Dogfish Woman appear to have been lost.

Perhaps one day we'll rediscover what the dogfish truly meant to the Haida. Until then, the high forehead, gill slits and sharp teeth of the heraldic dogfish crest can be seen on the new pole by Giitsxaa at Qay'llnagaay, and on his 1970 replica of a Skedans mortuary pole frontlet at the Skidegate cemetery. Dogfish Woman lives on in the iconography of the Haida, as well as in the art of Bill Reid and Robert Davidson, and in several famous Emily Carr paintings.

And she lives especially at the Haida Gwaii Museum, in a magnificent argillite carving of a dogfish transforming itself into a human female form. The artist, Gyaawhllns (also known as John Robson), would certainly have been familiar with the scene at the Oil Works, as he was born about 1850 and lived in Skidegate.

Having immersed ourselves in dogfish lore, we drive to the west coast of Graham Island, a fearsomely rugged area pierced by scores of inlets, uninhabited, wild, nearly roadless—the wettest and windiest region in Canada. On the entire western shoreline of Haida Gwaii there's only one place that can reasonably be reached by vehicle: Rennell Sound. Naturally, we can't resist going there.

Rennell is not that hard to get to. First you must enter Graham's labyrinthine logging road system, starting near Queen Charlotte City. To avoid becoming a logging-truck pancake, it's worth checking with the BC Forest Service before proceeding into this industrial heartland. There's a well-marked side road to Rennell Sound twenty-two kilometres along the mainline. Purple shooting stars dot the high meadows as we cross the mountains and begin the steep descent to the west coast. The total distance from the Skidegate ferry terminus is only about forty kilometres.

The sound itself, with its pebble and dark sand beaches, is spectacular even in poor weather. Its outer section receives the full brunt of the open Pacific; the inner part, Shields Bay, is more sheltered, while the head of the sound, known as Clapp Basin, is usually calm. Substantial mountains, still thickly capped with snow in mid-June, rise from the ocean to the south and west. In fact, Mount La Perouse, the apex of the massif that dominates the southern skyline, is Haida Gwaii's third-highest peak at 1,120 metres. It's also the high point of Graham Island.

It's overcast the day we arrive, though to the west, just offshore, the sky is a tempting blue. Low cloud banks keep forming along the coast and sailing eastward, offering glimpses of

THE BLOWHOLE AT THE BASE OF TOW HILL ON GRAHAM ISLAND

sunny alpine scenery as they drift along. We settle in at a Forest Service campsite on Shields Bay. Fishermen seem to be the main visitors here; several are well established, with heated prospector tents, showers and generator-powered freezers.

We launch our kayaks and paddle around Shields Bay and Clapp Basin, where one can explore numerous reef-fringed islands. Early in the century, a wharf and fish-buying station were located in the basin. Later came a logging camp, now converted to a private fishing resort; all day long small boats whiz back and forth to the entrance of Rennell Sound in search of giant halibut. On the southwest shore of Shields Bay, the remains of the Haida village of Lanahilduns could be seen until the 1920s.

The next day is drizzly and cold, and we soon talk ourselves out of paddling. Instead, we drive further west through evergreen tunnels along a logging road. The slopes round the sound show dozens of old clear-cuts, many of which have greened up in alder and may not have been replanted properly, if at all. At least one patch of old growth survives along Riley Creek. A lovely 2.5-kilometre trail has been built from the road to Riley Beach through groves of enormous Sitka spruce. Everything is draped in moss and studded with tree fungi. Few people hike there; the only tracks are those of deer and raccoons.

At the beach—a windswept spot pounded in winter by fierce storms—we search for fancy flotsam. Bottles with Japanese and Korean labels are plentiful. I discover a nifty fishnet float in blue plastic, festooned with gooseneck barnacles. With its Japanese printing and stylized fish design, it makes an excellent souvenir. Early visitors reported finding strange things—dried seahorses, coconuts, palm trees—on the sound's lonely beaches.

North of Riley Creek, we check out Gregory Beach, which has more Forest Service campsites, and Bonanza Beach, then drive back to camp and take a leisurely walk southward along the shoreline. In 1885, Jimmy Shields staked out a townsite here. Coal was to be brought in by rail and loaded onto ships. The railway route was surveyed, but the scheme came to nothing. All that remains is Shields's name on local landmarks.

After our stroll we meet the neighbours. One pair of fishermen show us a fifty-eight-kilogram halibut they've strapped to the back of their boat. The day before they had caught a ninety-kilogram monster. They are there for two weeks and will probably haul in at least half a tonne of fish. What can they do with so much? Nice guys, they offer fresh halibut to everyone on the beach. We sauté ours with a little basil, salt and pepper.

That evening the sun comes out and we go for a late paddle. As we cruise along, Katherine spies an unusual patch of turbulence ahead. It's a pod of Pacific white-sided dolphins. "Let's go!" she cries, her paddle twirling like a folk-art whirligig. I follow, not utterly convinced I want to be smack in the middle of twenty large, excited marine mammals. The pod halts a hundred metres from us and goes into a fifteen-minute feeding frenzy, with dolphins leaping out of the air again and again. It's electrifying to watch them from a kayak—a dramatic finale to our west coast visit.

From Rennell Sound we head back to Queen Charlotte City, then north on Highway 16 along the east coast of the island, past former agricultural communities such as Hydah and Lawn Hill, established in the early 1900s. At Hydah, the store was owned by William Leary, who originally came to the islands as manager of the Oil Works. Lawn Hill sported a store, as well, and a hotel, a Dominion Wireless Service station and an experimental farm run by the East Coast Farmer's Institute. Next up is Tlell, founded in 1904 by William Thomas Hodges, better known as Mexican Tom; a post office and general store still endure here, along with the Richardson Ranch. Just beyond is Naikoon Provincial Park, which covers the entire northeast corner of Graham Island.

POLE AND PAINTED LONGHOUSE AT OLD MASSET, GRAHAM ISLAND

Pitching our tent at Misty Meadows, one of two forty-site campgrounds in Naikoon, we prepare a meal. The intermittent rain slowly settles into a steady downpour. By the time the park operator comes around to collect our money, we're eating dinner under the firewood shelter, seated on rounds of Sitka spruce.

"Where is everyone?" he asks, half-seriously. It's Friday night, early summer: prime tourist time, you'd think, despite the unpredictable weather. We'd been worried that Misty Meadows would be full, but only three sites are occupied, including ours. In truth, there are few automobiles on the archipelago's 125 kilometres of pavement (and fewer still on the gravel roads, most of which are the private domain of the forest industry). The ferry runs six times a week in summer (half that in low season) and only carries eighty vehicles; reservations must be made far in advance. Many visitors rent cars in Haida Gwaii—or else hitchhike.

After dinner, with the weather deteriorating rapidly, I wander out to the beach. Huge waves are building in the rising storm. The dunes are covered with the pale blue blossoms of seashore lupin. Semi-palmated plovers careen in the wind; as they drop to the beach they disappear from sight, their colours blending perfectly into the background of sand and stone.

Nestled into a protective screen of shore pines, we survive the night without damage and move out after breakfast for a walk along East Beach. At seventy kilometres, this must be the longest beach in BC—and one of the longest in North America. You can hike the whole thing, fording rivers and gingerly skirting wave-washed headlands. Or you can risk your four-wheel-drive vehicle on its hard-packed sands. We're content to stroll out to the remains of the *Pesuta*, an eight-kilometre round trip that takes us three hours.

The trail first meanders for a kilometre or so along a forested ridge above the Tlell River. Purple fairyslipper orchids bloom at our feet along with fragrant white wax-flowers. A pair of red-breasted sapsuckers flits between the spruces. Down the beach, the huge timbers of the *Pesuta*, an eighty-metre log carrier that ran aground in December 1928, eventually come into sight. At the wreck, we eat packed lunches and enjoy the sweeping views before heading back.

The drive to North Beach on the other side of the park is long and circuitous. The weather is clearing, though; sunshine may even be in store. The highway leads inland from Tlell, away from Naikoon park, crossing a boggy landscape of scrub trees, western swamp-laurel and Labrador tea. Eventually, it runs north to the shores of Masset Sound and the town of

Masset, then east and back into Naikoon via a well-travelled twenty-kilometre gravel road.

On the north coast of Graham Island, from Masset to Rose Spit, another stupendous array of beaches stretches for forty kilometres. The spit itself, an ecological reserve, sticks out three kilometres into the ocean—and as far again underwater. Without a vehicle (or a bicycle), it's a twenty-kilometre hike from the end of the road to this treeless finger of sand.

As we settle in at spectacular Agate Beach campground, I beseech my mate to help me resist the urge to take our truck onto the sands. A stiff wind is blowing off Dixon Entrance, dispersing clouds and ushering in a major sunset and a ridge of high pressure that will bless us with two days of sunshine. That time is spent leisurely exploring the beaches and network of trails that lead from nearby Tow Hill across the Argonaut Plain, with its sphagnum bogs and weird, insect-eating plants, to East Beach.

From the hill's summit, we take in enormous views. Below us, a cavalcade of vehicles sets off toward the spit. Tow Hill, an exposed volcanic extrusion of columnar basalt, has been carved away at its base into a gallery of unusual shapes and a fantastic blowhole, where the waves surge through a narrow archway. On Agate Beach, solitary rock-hunters, their heads bent over, eyes glued to the ground, stroll the shining strand.

One morning, as an early mist evaporates in the sun, a sheepish fellow, dishevelled and hungover, makes the rounds of the campground looking for a ride into Masset. His buddy hangs back by the road, accompanied by a large dog. Yup, their truck is stuck way out on North Beach, where a stream has softened the sand. They're looking at a very expensive tow—or a complete vehicular write-off—but they find a ride into town, at least.

The next day, it's time to head back south, past the Delkatla Wildlife Refuge (shorebirds and waterfowl; sandhill cranes, if you're lucky) and through Masset, where skid-row ravens, oblivious to traffic, beg without shame on the main street. We stop for lattes at a specialty coffee shop named Haidabucks and make a side trip to the adjacent Haida community of Old Masset, an ancient settlement site, with its crafts shops and poles.

Near Pure Lake Provincial Park a detour leads to the mouth of Watun River, where a cannery operated in the 1920s. Nothing is left. The tiny village of Port Clements makes a good lunch stop; there's a fascinating little museum there devoted to the history of the forest industry. Near Juskatla, a logging community, a side road that turns into a trail ends with a remarkable sight: an unfinished dugout canoe, who knows how old, partially shaped from a fallen cedar and then left to rot after the discovery of some fatal flaw.

By now the rains have resumed, so back at Queen Charlotte City it's time for a treat: a night at Gracie's Place, a friendly hotel with cooking facilities. After a last visit to Qay'llnagaay, where we see young Haida women wearing smart, finely woven spruce-root hats, we get in line to board the *Queen of Prince Rupert* for the trip back to the mainland. Behind us, Skidegate is preparing for Graham Island's latest party: a potlatch in honour of the fiftieth wedding anniversary of Chief Skidegate and his wife. On Haida Gwaii, it seems, the good times keep on rolling.

THE DOCK AT SOUTH WINCHELSEA ISLAND LOOKING WEST TO VANCOUVER ISLAND

Ballenas-Winchelsea

The delights of a tiny archipelago

From Schooner Cove, Lyle Montgomery runs us over to the Winchelsea group in his water taxi. As he rounds the navy buoy just south of the islands we see the animals, scores of them, littering the rocks like a broken boom of short, fat logs. Next we hear them, a chorus of barks and growls that merge to form a dull roar. They lift their massive heads to watch us but don't budge one centimetre from their perches.

"Wait 'til you smell 'em," says Lyle, but the wind, for now, is not co-operating. The objects of our attention are a hundred or so fully grown male California and Steller's sea lions spread out along the shore. Not 300 metres away, on a separate island, is the cabin we're headed toward. For the next three days (and nights), the sea lions' antics and bellowed conversations will entertain us as we explore our surroundings by kayak and foot.

It's the end of March, mild but gusty, and Katherine and I are visiting South Winchelsea Island off Nanoose Bay on Vancouver Island with our friends Mike and Elaine. The Ballenas-Winchelsea archipelago may not be a well-known kayaking destination, but on the chart, at least, its nineteen islands look perfect for paddling. The only drawback might be the fact that we're within spitting distance of Whiskey Golf, the navy's controversial torpedo testing range. A monitoring station on North Winchelsea Island, only half a kilometre from the cabin, bristles with antennae, aerials, satellite dishes and a bright orange-and-white dome. If you paddle too close, we hear, naval personnel will emerge and shout at you to stay clear.

This early in the season the weather is marginal for paddling, but that's the beauty of South Winchelsea. The three-bedroom Robert T. Ogilvie Research Cottage is quite comfortable; if you can't get out on the water, just stay close to home and explore the 10.4-hectare island or else put your feet up in front of the fire. Both cabin and island are owned by The Land Conservancy of BC (TLC), a non-profit organization that works to protect sensitive and endangered ecosystems *(www.conservancy.bc.ca)*. In 1998, in partnership with two other land trusts, TLC purchased South Winchelsea for $595,000. Now, having methodically paid off a $445,000 mortgage, it's working to restore the island's rare and unusual Garry oak-arbutus ecosystem to its original state.

TLC owns, manages or holds covenants on dozens of ecologically valuable properties around the province, from the Abkhazi Gardens in Victoria to the Koeye River Valley near Bella Bella and Linnaea Farm on Cortes Island. Several can bear a certain amount of carefully measured human traffic and have habitable structures on them, which TLC rents out to raise funds for its acquisition and restoration programs. Visitors can stay at cabins on the Cowichan River, near Sooke and beside Nimpo Lake in the Chilcotin, but the one on South Winchelsea, with its rainwater-collection system, solar panels and well-equipped kitchen, may be the nicest of the lot.

We head out in our kayaks the morning after we arrive and paddle round our island home. The wind is rising from the southeast, though, and steep waves are beginning to form, so next we investigate more protected waters between North and South Winchelsea, keeping well away from the boisterous pinnipeds. A dozen immature bald eagles swirl above us, while Vancouver Island's 1,817-metre Mount Arrowsmith glistens in the background. The afternoon is devoted to exploring the island, where spring wildflowers—blue-eyed Mary, sea blush, shootingstar, chocolate lily, chickweed monkey-flower and common camas—are starting to bloom. A mink grooms itself on a sunny driftwood log.

We've never had the opportunity before to observe so many sea lions at such close range, and we spend hours watching them through binoculars. It's not difficult to distinguish the two species: the Stellers, endangered and in decline throughout their range, are enormous (up to a tonne), lighter coloured and in the minority here; the more abundant Californias, whose population is increasing, are sleeker, much smaller (a mere 350 kilos) and rich chocolate in hue. No one knows exactly why the Stellers are in such bad shape; disease, pollution and reduced food sources as a result of commercial fisheries are all believed to be contributing factors.

Steller's sea lions live year-round in BC waters, while adult male Californias arrive on the southern coast in late fall and winter. Males of both species hang together until about April, at which time they migrate to their respective breeding

ROBERT T. OGILVIE RESEARCH COTTAGE ON SOUTH WINCHELSEA

grounds (Mexico and the southern US for the Californias; Queen Charlotte Sound or farther north for the Stellers). The animals we watch seem to spend most of their time sleeping, with occasional forays into the ocean. When one wishes to climb back up on the rocks and make a space for itself among its fellows, all hell breaks loose: necks arch and teeth are bared; horrid groans issue forth from big pink mouths. We go out to the water's edge in order to get as close a view as possible and are engulfed with the fetid odours of decaying fish.

In the evenings, over bottles of red wine, braised tofu and asparagus, chicken stir-fry and other pleasant-smelling foods, we amuse ourselves with fantasies about testing North Winchelsea's security measures at night. Staff, for instance, would be surprised to awaken and find "Osama was here" sprayed on their compound walls. Then we consider that our neighbours might just be amusing themselves by listening in on our conversations with impossibly high-tech eavesdropping devices. So how far do you think those Canucks will get in the hockey playoffs, anyway?

The next day is sunny but very windy and we remain island-bound. In Whiskey Golf, officially known as the Canadian Forces Maritime Experimental Test Range, small ships plough back and forth. Helicopters hover and lift things from the ocean, while a gigantic US Navy plane flies endless, low circles overhead. Over 500 air-, ship- and submarine-launched torpedoes are tested annually in this eight by twenty-four-kilometre zone, as well as sonar, sonobuoys and other maritime war gear. Foreign governments, especially the US, frequently use the range.

The province owns the sea floor beneath the Strait of Georgia and until 1999 had a licence agreement with Canada allowing Whiskey Golf to be used as a test facility. When that agreement expired, the two governments tried to negotiate a lease renewal, but talks broke down over the issue of nuclear warheads. Ottawa, after conferring with the US, refused to prohibit them and eventually expropriated the 217 square kilometres of seafloor that it needed. In a series of public hearings in 1999, thousands of individuals filed written objections and made presentations opposing this first hostile expropriation of provincial land in Canadian history. But to no avail;

at the end of the year, Canada announced a ten-year extension of its agreement with the US Navy for use of the range.

Back on South Winchelsea, we wait out the wind by working our way completely around the island's rocky perimeter, taking care not to trample vegetation or damage fragile moss and lichen gardens. There is plenty of birdlife on the island, we notice, and some species, including the yellow-rumped warbler, are arrayed in breeding plumage. Fox sparrows, rufous towhees, northern flickers and belted kingfishers swoop and call.

I cast yearning glances at the rest of the archipelago, which we will not be reaching, it appears, on this journey. Only four islands—Gerald, Maude, Mistaken and South Winchelsea—are privately owned, and none are permanently inhabited. The islands have never been grazed by cattle or browsed by deer, and have seen little human disturbance, which makes them especially valuable reservoirs of biodiversity. Local conservationists are hopeful that more—and perhaps all—of the group can be protected.

The largest islands, across a three-kilometre-wide channel, are East and West Ballenas, named by early Spanish explorers after the region's once-bountiful whales. East Ballenas, owned by the Department of National Defence, has a lovely beach and is home to a rare plant, the water-plantain buttercup. West Ballenas is the site of a lighthouse station, destaffed in 1996. For early keepers—including William Brown, who went mad there in 1906 and was committed to an asylum, and Arthur Gurney, a troublemaking alcoholic whose departmental file bulged with complaints—it was a dreary spot. Their successors enjoyed station life, though; they could be in Parksville by boat in twenty minutes. The last keeper, Richard Wood, interviewed by author Lynn Tanod for a book called

SOUTH WINCHELSEA'S OGILVIE COTTAGE SET IN A GROVE OF GARRY OAKS

Guiding Lights just before he and his wife, Reta, transferred to Cape Scott, called it "a breeze—an old man's station, really."

Our final morning is a breeze, as well. It breaks calm and clear, and we get in a magnificent paddle around the nearby Ada Islands, where patches of new foliage and spring colour brighten up the stone. Harlequin ducks, black oystercatchers, pelagic cormorants and black turnstones go about their business. Dozens of seals pop their heads out of the water to check on our progress. Soon it's time to clean up and pack up. Next thing we know Lyle and his water taxi are running a gauntlet of disapproving sea lions to return us, reluctantly, to our everyday lives.

Index

Photographs are in **boldface.**
* indicates a photo in the unpaginated colour section.